The Writings of the Last Generation
&
The Nation

The Writings of the Last Generation & The Nation

LAITMAN
KABBALAH
PUBLISHERS

Rav Yehuda Ashlag

The Writings of the Last Generation
&
The Nation

Published by Laitman Kabbalah Publishers

www.bundleofreeds.com   contact@bundleofreeds.com

1057 Steeles Avenue West, Suite 532, Toronto,
ON, M2R 3X1, Canada

2009 85th Street #51, Brooklyn, New York, 11214, USA

Printed in Canada

ISBN: 978-1-77228-006-7

Library of Congress Control Number: 2015909641

Proof Reading: Mary Miesem

Copy Editor: Mary Pennock

Layout: Eugene Nemirovsky, Chaim Ratz

Cover: Inna Smirnova

Translation: Chaim Ratz

Printing and Post Production: Uri Laitman

FIRST EDITION: SEPTEMBER 2015

First Printing

Table of Contents

Editor's Note..7

The Writings of the Last Generation.............................9
    Introduction to the Writings of the Last Generation.....11
    Part One..15
        Appendices and Drafts...51
    Part Two..81
    Part Three...101
    Part Four...115
    Part Five...125

The Nation...141

    Detailed Table of Contents.......................................187
    Further Reading...191
    Contact Information..200

Editor's Note

The original manuscripts of these writings are stored in the ARI Institute archive.

The publication process was quite complicated due to the condition of the manuscripts, and because of the great density of the texts. First, we located all the writings that belong to the "Writings of the Last Generation" by their content. Subsequently, we meticulously copied the texts without any corrections of typos or editing. Where we could not decipher a word or part of a word, we marked it with ellipses [...].

We divided the writings into five parts and an introduction, according to their appearance in the manuscripts. It should be noted that the ordering of the parts was done by us. All the titles in the writings were given by Baal HaSulam himself, and where marking a title had to be added we used only the ABC letters.

We should pay close attention to the lion share in "The Writings of the Last Generation," Part One. According to the manuscript, the material is in fact divided into two: 1) Essay, 2) Appendices and drafts of the essay.

The Editor

The Writings of the Last Generation

Introduction to the Writings of the Last Generation

There is an allegory about friends who were lost in the desert, hungry and thirsty. One of them had found a settlement filled abundantly with every delight. He remembered his poor brothers, but he had already drawn far off from them and did not know where they were. What did he do? He began to shout out loud and blow the horn; perhaps his poor hungry friends would hear his voice, approach him, and come to that abundant settlement that is filled with every delight.

So is the matter before us: We have been lost in the terrible desert along with all of humanity, and now we have found a great, abundant treasure, namely the books of Kabbalah in the treasure. They satisfy our yearning souls and fill us abundantly with lushness and contentment; we are satiated and there is more.

Yet, we remember our friends, who were left hopelessly in the terrible desert. There is a great distance between us, and words cannot bridge it. For this reason, we have set up this horn to blow out loud so that our brothers might hear and draw near and be as happy as we.

Know, our brothers, our flesh, that the essence of the wisdom of Kabbalah is the knowledge of how the world came down from its elevated, heavenly place, until it reached our ignoble state. This reality was necessary, as "the

11

end of an act is in the initial thought," and His thought acts instantaneously, for He needs no tools to work with as we do. Thus, we were emanated in Infinity in utter perfection from the start, and from there we came to this world.

It is therefore very easy to find all the future corrections, which are destined to come, from the perfect worlds that preceded us. Through it we know how to correct our ways henceforth, like man's advantage over the beast, where the spirit of the beast descends, meaning sees only from itself onward, without the intellect or wisdom to look into the past so as to correct the future.

Man's advantage over it is that the spirit of man ascends into the past, and looks into the past as one looks in the mirror and sees one's flaws so as to correct them. Similarly, the mind sees what it has been through, and corrects its future conducts.

Thus, beasts do not evolve; they are still, in the same state in which they were created, for they do not have, as man does, the mirror by which to see how to correct things and gradually evolve. Man develops day-by-day until his merit is secured and sensed, and he will ride on the high planets.

But all this refers to the natures outside of us, the nature of our surrounding reality, our food and mundane affairs. For this, the natural mind is quite sufficient.

However, internally, in our selves, although we do evolve some, we evolve and improve by being pushed from behind through suffering and bloodshed. It is so because we have no tactic by which to obtain a mirror to see inside man, which they had in past generations.

It is even more so regarding the interior of the souls and the worlds, and how they came to such dreadful ruin as today's, where we have no safety in our lives. We will be subject to all sorts of slaughter and death in the coming years, and all admit that they have no counsel to prevent it.

Imagine, for example, that some historic book were to be found today, depicting the last generations ten thousand years from now. As we feel, the lesson from the suffering and torment will certainly be enough to reform them in a good manner.

And these people have before them good orders, sufficient to provide certainty and complacency. And at the very least, to guarantee their daily lives in peace and quiet.

There is no doubt that if some sage would offer us this book about the wisdom of policy and personal conduct, our leaders would seek out every counsel to arrange life accordingly, and there would be "no outcry in our broad places." Corruption and the terrible suffering would cease, and everything would come peacefully to its place.

Now, distinguished readers, this book lies here before you in a closet. It states explicitly all the wisdom of statesmanship and the conducts of private and public life that will exist at the end of days, meaning the books of Kabbalah [in the manuscript, beside the text beginning here, it was written, "They are the perfection preceding imperfection"]. In it, the corrected worlds that emerged with perfection are set, as it says, perfection emerges first from the Creator, then we correct it and come to the perfection existing in the Upper World, emerging from *Ein Sof* [infinity], as in, "the end of an act is in the initial thought." Because the incomplete extends gradually from the complete, and there is no absence in the spiritual, they all remain existing and depicted in their complete perfection, in particular and in general, in the wisdom of Kabbalah.

Open these books and you will find all the good orders that will appear and the end of days, and you will find within them the good lesson by which to arrange mundane matters today as well, for we can learn from the past and by that correct the future.

A Call for the Chosen Ones to Study Kabbalah

I, the writer, know myself and my place, that I am not among the finest in the human species. And if one such as me today has labored and found all this in the books concealed within our cabinets, there is not a shadow of a doubt that if the chosen ones in the generation delve in these books, so much of the happiness and bounty will be available for them and for the entire world.

My Voice that Is in the *Shofar* [Horn], Why Has It Come?

I have seen all that, and I can no longer restrain myself. I have resolved to disclose of my observations and of what I have found written in those books, regarding the conducts of correction of our definite future. And I go out and call upon the people of the world with this horn. I do believe and estimate that it shall suffice to gather all the chosen ones to begin to study and delve in the books, so they may sentence themselves and the entire world to a scale of merit.

Part One

The basis of my entire commentary is the will to receive that is imprinted in every creature, and which is disparity of form to the Creator. Thus, the soul has separated from Him as an organ is separated from the body, since disparity of form in spirituality is like a separating axe in corporeality. It is therefore clear that what the Creator wants from us is equivalence of form, at which time we cleave to Him once more, as before we were created.

Our sages said: "Cleave unto His attributes; as He is merciful, etc." It means that we are to change our attribute, which is the will to receive, and adopt the attribute of the Creator, which is only to bestow, so that all our actions will be only to bestow upon our fellow persons and benefit them as best as we can.

By that we come to the goal of cleaving unto Him, which is equivalence of form. What one is compelled to do for oneself, namely the necessary minimum for one's self and one's family's sustenance, is not considered disparity of form, as "Necessity is neither condemned nor praised." This is the great revelation that will only be revealed entirely in the days of the Messiah. When this teaching is received, we will be rewarded with complete redemption.

I have already said that there are two ways to discover the completeness: the path of Torah or the path of suffering.

Hence, the Creator has given humanity technology, until they have invented the atom and the hydrogen bombs. If the total ruin that they are destined to bring upon the world is still not evident to the world, they can wait for a third world war, or a fourth one. The bombs will do their thing and the relics that remain after the ruin will have no other choice but to take upon themselves this work, where both individuals and nations will not work for themselves more than is necessary for their sustenance, while everything else they do will be for the good of others. If all the nations of the world agree to it, there will no longer be wars in the world, for no person will be concerned with his own good whatsoever, but only with the good of others.

This law of equivalence of form is the law of the Messiah. It is said about that (Micah 4): "But in the end of days it shall come to pass, and many nations shall go and say: 'Come, and let us go up for out of Zion shall go forth the law, and He shall judge between many nations.'" That is, the Messiah will teach them the work of God in equivalence of form, which is the teaching and the law of the Messiah. "And shall prove to mighty nations," meaning He will prove to them that if they do not take upon themselves the work of God, all nations will be destroyed by war. However, if they do accept His law, it is said about it, "and they shall beat their swords into shovels."

If you take the path of Torah, and receive the spice, very well. And if you do not, you will tread the path of suffering, meaning that wars will break out with atom and hydrogen bombs, and the entire world will seek counsel to escape the war. Then they shall come to the Messiah, to Jerusalem, and He will teach them this law.

*

Before I touch upon this matter, I will present a short introduction concerning human attributes, and say that people are divided into two kinds: egoists and altruists.

Egoists means that all that they do is for themselves. And if they ever do something for another, they must have a well-paying reward in return for their work, in money, respect, etc.

Altruists means that they sacrifice all their days for the well-being of others, without any reward. Instead, they always neglect their own needs to help others. Moreover, among them there are such who give their souls and their lives to the benefit of others, such as those we find among volunteers who go out to war for their countryfolk.

We have also found more general altruists, meaning those who give their hearts and souls to help the backward of all the nations of the world, such as communists, who fight for the benefit of oppressed among all the nations of the world. They are willing to pay for it with their very life.

Egoism is embedded in the nature of every person, as in any animal. Altruism, however, is against human nature. Yet, a chosen few are imparted this nature; I call them "idealists." Yet, the majority of any society or state is made of simple flesh and blood folk, meaning egoists. Only a few, ten percent at most, are the exceptional altruists.

Now I shall come to the point: For the above reason, that altruists are so few in every society, the first communists, before Karl Marx's time, were unsuccessful in acting toward spreading communism in the world, as in the saying, "One bird doesn't make a summer." In addition, some of them even established communal settlements like the kibbutzim in our country, but they failed because they could not endure.

This happened because all the members of the communal society must be altruistic idealists, as the founders themselves. Since ninety percent of any society, even the most developed, are egoists, they could not keep up with the conducts of a cooperative society, which is purely altruistic by nature.

This continued until the time of Karl Marx, when a very successful plan for the expansion of communism was devised, namely to incorporate the oppressed themselves in the war of communism, so that they would fight alongside them against the capitalistic bourgeois government. Since the oppressed are interested in this war only for their own good, meaning for egoistic reasons, they immediately accepted the plan, and thus communism spread out among all the levels of the backward and the oppressed. Since the backward are the majority in society, it is no surprise that today communism has succeeded in encircling a third of the world.

However, this coupling of the altruist communists with the egoistic proletariat, though it was successful in overthrowing the bourgeois government, hateful to both, that coupling still fails to keep a cooperative government with just division. The reason is very simple: A person does not make a move unless there is some purpose that necessitates that movement. That purpose serves as the motivating force to make that move like fuel that moves a machine.

For example, one does not move his hand from one place to another unless he thinks that in the other place he will be more comfortable resting his hand. That purpose of seeking a more comfortable place for one's hand is the fuel pushing his hand from this place to the other.

Needless to say, a worker who labors all day must have fuel for the laborious movements he makes. The reward for his work is the fuel that motivates him to his hard work. Thus, if no reward is given for his labor, or if he has no need for that reward, he will not be able to work. He will be like a machine that was not fueled; even the most gullible person in the world will not think that this machine will ever move.

Hence, in a purely communistic regime, where the worker knows that he will not be given more if he works more, or receive less if he works less, and all the more so in light of the absolute motto, "Each will work according to his ability and receive according to his needs," the worker will neither be rewarded for his diligence, nor fear his own negligence.

Thus, he would have no fuel to motivate him to work. The labor productivity of the workers would then drop to zero, until they ruin the entire regime. No schooling in the world will help in inverting human nature to be able to work without fuel, meaning without reward.

The exception to this rule is the natural born altruist idealist for whom the best reward is the good of the other. This altruistic fuel is entirely sufficient for him as a motivating force to work, like the egoistic reward for all other people. However, idealists are few; their number is insufficient for society to base itself on them. Thus, you see that communism and altruism are one and the same.

I know there are ways to compel workers to complete their share of the work that the supervisors will give them by the same conducts as in a bourgeois government, where each is rewarded according to his productivity. In addition, harsh punishment can be imposed on the negligent, as in soviet countries. However, this is not communism whatsoever. Needless to say, it is not the paradise that the communist regime is hoped to bring about, one worthy of giving one's life for.

Moreover, a government such as this is far worse than the bourgeois government for unambiguous reasons that I will present below. Had that compulsive government been a step toward the perfect communism, it would still have been acceptable and tolerable. However, that is not the case; no training in the world will reverse human nature from egoism to altruism.

Therefore, the oppressive regime applied in the soviet countries is an eternal regime that can never be changed. And when they desire to change it into a truly cooperative regime, the workers will run out of fuel. They will not be able to work and will destroy the government. Thus, egoism and anti-communism are one and the same, identical.

Moreover, a compulsive communist government is completely unsustainable, since a bayonet-dependent government cannot persist, and the majority will ultimately rise against it and abolish it. The idealist ten percent will not be able to rule over the egoistic ninety percent and the anti-communists forever. This is what we find in soviet and eastern countries.

Moreover, even that handful of communist idealists that lead these countries today are not guaranteed to stay that way for generations, since ideals are not hereditary. Although the progenitors are idealists, there is no guarantee that their progeny will follow suit.

Thus, how can we be certain that the leadership of the second or third generation will be in the hands of communist idealists as it is today? You might say that the majority will always elect them from the public, but this is a grave mistake. The majority of the egoistic public will elect only those who are close to them in spirit, not their opponents.

Moreover, it is common knowledge that today's leaders were not elected by the public at all. Thus, who would make certain that the elected representatives of the public will always be the idealists in the public? When the egoists are in power, they are sure to revoke that government instantaneously, or at least turn it into a kind of national communism, "a nation of Lords."

All that I have said—when I proved that communism and altruism are the same, and that egoism and anti-communism are the same—is my own view. However, if you ask the communists themselves, they will deny it vehemently. They will claim the opposite: "We are far from any bourgeois ethics; we have no sentimentalism. It is only justice that we seek, that no man shall exploit another." In other words, it is according to the attribute, "what's mine is mine, and what's yours is yours," which is, in fact, the attribute of egoists. Hence, I must view the matters from their perceptive, and review this justice that they seek and to which they devote their lives.

First, according to the development of the communist regimes, I find that the terms, "bourgeois" and "proletariat," are no longer sufficient to explain that economic history, and we need more general terms. It is truer to divide society into a class of diligent and a class of backward. In the bourgeois regimes, the diligent are the capitalists and the middle class. The backward are the workers who labor for them. In the communist regimes, the diligent are the managers, the supervisors, and the intellectuals, and the backward are the workers who labor for them.

The majority in every society is always the backward. The diligent are no more than thirty percent of society. It is a natural law that the diligent class will exploit the backward class as best they can, like fish at sea, where the strong swallows the weak. It is inconsequential whether the diligent are capitalists and merchants, as in the bourgeois regimes, or whether the diligent are the managers, supervisors, the intellectuals, and the allotters, as in the communist regimes.

Ultimately, the diligent will exploit the laboring backward to the best of their ability; they will take no pity on them. The diligent will always suck out the butter and the cream, leaving the workers with only the meager whey. The only question is what remains for the workers after the ruthless exploitation by the diligent, the measure of enslavement the diligent impose on them, and the measure of freedom and human liberty the diligent allow them. It is only according to the measure of these leftovers, which the diligent leave for the backward, that we are to examine every regime, differentiate between the regimes, and choose which one is preferable.

Let us mention once more what we said, that one cannot work without any reward that serves as a fuel for a machine.

In a non-altruistic communist regime, the workers must be rewarded for their work, and be heavily punished for their negligence.

However, many supervisors are required to watch over them, for without sufficient supervision, the rewards and punishments are certain to be insufficient. However, there is no harder work than standing over people and agonizing them, for "no one wants to be a hangman." Hence, even if you place inspectors, appointees over the inspectors, and higher still appointees to watch them, they will all be negligent in their supervision, and they will not agonize the workers sufficiently.

There is no cure for that except to provide plenty of fuel to the functionaries, sufficient as reward for such hard labor, meaning the work of the hangman. In other words, they must be given several times more than a simple worker.

Thus, you should not be surprised if functionaries in Russia are paid ten to fifty times more than a simple worker; their work is ten to fifty times harder than that of a simple worker. If they are not sufficiently rewarded, they will be compelled to neglect their office, and the state will be ruined.

Now try to calculate in our country's currency. Let us say that a simple worker earns a hundred Israeli pounds a month. This means that the lowest functionaries will receive a thousand pounds a month, ten times more. Thus, over one year, he will earn twelve thousand pounds, and over ten years, a hundred and twenty thousand pounds.

If we deduct ten percent from that for his sustenance, he will be left with a hundred and eight thousand pounds. It seems that we should consider him a respectable capitalist. It is even more so with the higher functionaries.

Thus, within a few decades, the functionaries will become millionaires, at no risk, but strictly through the exploitation of the workers. As I have said, by today's experience, society should no longer be divided into bourgeois and proletariat, but into the diligent and the backward.

You might say that this is but a phase toward pure communism, meaning that through education and public opinion, the public will be tutored until "each will work according to his ability and receive according to his needs." Then there will be no need for inspectors and supervisors.

This is a big mistake because the motto of each working according to his ability and receiving according to his needs is a strictly altruistic motto. Wherever one can work to the benefit of society without any fuel, it is unnatural, unless altruism is the reason and the fuel for the work, as I have demonstrated.

Thus, we must not hope for any change for the better. Quite the contrary, we must fear that that handful of idealist communists who are leading today will not bequeath their leadership to other idealists. The egoistic force of the people will gradually prevail, they will choose a leadership according to their egoistic spirit, and will reinstate capitalism. At the very least, they will turn communism into some sort of national communism, a "master nation," as did Hitler. They will have no inhibitions about exploiting other nations to benefit themselves, if they only have the power.

You might say that through education and public opinion, the nature of the masses can be turned to altruism, but this is also a grave mistake. Education can do no more than public opinion, meaning that public opinion will respect the altruists and despise the egoists.

24

As long as public opinion sustains altruism by means of respect and ignominy, education will be effective. However, if there comes a time when an experienced and competent speaker gives a daily speech that is the opposite of public opinion, he will undoubtedly succeed in changing public opinion as he wishes.

We already have such a bitter experience in history with that villain who turned a well-mannered people like the Germans into wild animals through his daily sermons. Several hundred years of education vanished like a soap bubble, since public opinion had changed, and education had nothing more to rely on, as education cannot exist without the public's support.

Thus, you evidently see that there is no hope to change this compulsive government. There is also no hope that the masses will ever achieve true communism, according to the motto, "Each will work according to his ability and receive according to his needs."

Rather, the workers must remain eternally under the dreadful rod of the managers and the supervisors, while the managers and supervisors will always suck the blood of the workers, as bourgeois capitalists do, if not much worse than they. After all, in the compulsory regime of the communists, the workers do not even have the right to strike. Famine and destruction will always hang over their heads, as the Soviet experience teaches. Moreover, if the compulsory government is ever revoked, society will certainly be ruined instantaneously, for the workers would run out of fuel.

Indeed ... It is said that in a communist regime it is worthwhile for the proletariat to suffer, since they suffer for themselves, as they are the owners of the productive means,

25

the property, and the surplus, and no one can exploit them. However, in a capitalist regime they only have their daily bread, and all the surplus is given to the capitalists. How lovely these words are on the surface.

Nevertheless, if there is an ounce of truth in these words, then they apply to the diligent, who are the functionaries and the managers, who take all the pleasures of the compulsory regime in any case. Indeed, regarding the proletariat, namely the workers and the backward, these are idle words entirely.

Let us take our own railroads, for example. They are state property, meaning that the ownership of the railroad is in the hands of all the citizens of the state. I ask, do any of us citizens feel our right to ownership of the railroad? Do we have any greater benefit when traveling on a nationalized railway when compared to traveling on a private, capitalistic railway?

We can also take a cooperative owned entirely by the proletariat, like Solel Boneh (a large construction corporation in Israel), owned solely by the workers. Do the workers who work in their own property have any additional benefit than when working for a foreign capitalistic property?

I fear that one who works for the foreign entrepreneur will feel much more at home than one working for Solel Boneh, even though he is seemingly a co-owner. Only the handful of managers has the entire ownership, and they do with the national property as they see fit. A private citizen is forbidden to even inquire what they are doing, and for what.

Thus, the proletariat feels no delight in the property of the state and the productive means that is under the hands of the executives and the functionaries, who always oppress and humiliate them as the dust of the earth. What then is the surplus that they have in the compulsory communist regime, more than their daily bread?

I do not envy the proletariat whatsoever. They are and always will be in the compulsory communist regime, under the harsh encumbrance of the functionaries and inspectors, who can torture them with all sorts of atrocities, oblivious to the world and to public opinion, as all the advertising mediums will be in the hands of the clerks. No one will be able to expose his or her evil deeds in public.

In addition, everyone will be bound under their hands, unable to leave the country and escape them, just as our fathers were locked in Egypt, where no slave could leave there to be free. Because all the workers leave the surplus of the produce for the state, how will they let them go elsewhere, when the state loses their surplus? In a word, a non-altruistic communist regime must always consist of two classes: the diligent, who are the managers, the functionaries, and the intellectuals, and the class of the backward, who are the productive workers, the majority of society.

For the functioning of the state, the class of the diligent must, willingly or unwillingly, enslave, tantalize, and humiliate the working class mercilessly and shamelessly. They will exploit them ten times more than the bourgeois exploit them, for they will be utterly defenseless, as they will not have the right to strike. They will be unable to disclose the evil deeds of the employers in public, and they will take no pleasure at all in the ownership of the productive means that the functionaries have acquired.

2) One more thing, and this is the most important. Communism must correct more than just the economic order. It must also ensure the minimal existence of the

people in the world. In other words, it is to prevent wars so that nations will not destroy one another. I have already screamed like a crane over it back in 1933, in my book, *The Peace* pamphlet, warning that wars today have come to such proportions that they endanger the life of the entire world.

The only counsel to prevent this is by all the nations adopting the regime of perfect communism, meaning altruistic. Needless to say, today, after the discovery and use of atom bombs, and the discovery of hydrogen bombs, it is no longer doubtful that after one, two, or three wars, the entire human civilization will be totally ruined, leaving no relics.

Contemporary, modern egoism cannot secure peace in the world, for even if all the nations of the world adopt this communist regime, there will still not be a compelling reason for nations rich in production means, raw materials, and civilization, to share the raw materials and productive means equally with the poor nations.

For example, the nations in America will not want to equalize their standard of living with the Asian or African nations, or even with the European nations. A single nation might have the power to equalize the standard of living of the rich and middleclass—the owners of the productive means—with the proletariat, by inciting the poor masses, the majority of society, to destroy the rich and middleclass and take their property. However, this counsel will not be of any use in compelling a wealthy nation to share its property and means of production with a poor nation, as the rich nation has already prepared arms and bombs to safeguard itself from its poor neighbors.

Thus, what good did the communistic regime do in the world? It leaves intact the state of envy among the nations just as in the capitalistic regime, without any relief. A just division within each nation for itself will not assist to just division among the nations whatsoever.

Hence, while basic sustenance is under such immediate risk, it is a waste of time to improve the economic government. They would be better off using that time seeking counsel to save the very life of all humankind.

You see that the whole problem with today's communistic regime is the lack of adequate reward, which is the fuel for the productive force of the workers. Hence, it is impossible to employ them successfully except with the fuel of reward and punishment.

Hence, we need inspectors, supervisors, and managers to take upon themselves this hard work of supervising the workers, and ruthlessly suck their blood and sweat, making their lives endlessly bitter with hardship and enslavement. In return for this hard work, they must also be given adequate reward, which is no less than to make them millionaires, for they will not want to live the life of hangmen of their own free will for any less than that, as we see in the Soviet country.

In addition, we must not hope for this reign of terror to ever end, as the optimists promise. Neither bayonets nor education or public opinion will be able to change human nature to work willingly without adequate fuel.

Hence, it is a curse for generations. When the compulsory government is revoked, the workers will no longer yield a produce that will suffice for the sustenance of the state. There is no cure for that, except to bring faith in spiritual reward and punishment from above into the hearts of the workers, from He who knows all mysteries.

Thus, through the right education and promotion, the spiritual reward and punishment will be sufficient fuel for the produce of their work. They will no longer need managers or supervisors over their shoulders, but each and every one will work willingly and wholeheartedly for society, to win his or her reward from Heaven.

THE POSITIVE

1. Communism is an ideal, meaning moral. The goal "to work according to one's ability and receive according to one's needs" testifies to that.

2. Every moral must have a basis that necessitates it; education and public opinion are a very unsound basis, and the proof of this is Hitler.

3. Because any concept of the majority is sure to triumph, it is needless to say that the carrying out of the corrected communism is by the majority of the public. Thus, it is necessary to establish the moral level of the majority of the public on a basis that will necessitate and guarantee that the corrected communism will never be corrupted. The preordained ideal in humans is insufficient, as too few possess it, and they are insignificant compared to the majority of the public.

4. Religion is the only basis sure to raise the level of the collective to the moral level of "working according to the ability and receiving according to the need."

5. Communism must be turned away from the concept, "What's mine is mine and what's yours is yours," which is sodomite rule, to the concept,

"What's mine is yours and what's yours is yours," meaning absolute altruism. When the majority of the public accepts this rule *de facto*, it will be time to "work according to the ability and receive according to the need." The sign would be that every one would work like a contract-worker.

6. It is forbidden to nationalize property before the public reaches this moral level. Before there is a reliable moral factor in the public, the collective will not have fuel for work.

7. The entire world is one family. The framework of communism should ultimately encircle the entire world in an equal standard of living for all. However, the actual process is a gradual one. Each nation whose majority accepts these basic elements practically, and has a guaranteed fuel, may enter the framework of communism right away.

8. The economic and religious form that guarantees communism will be the same for all nations. Except for religious forms, which do not concern the economy and other conducts, each will have one's own form, which must not be changed at all.

9. The world must not be corrected in religious matters before economic correction is guaranteed for the entire world.

10. There should be a detailed program from all the above-mentioned rules and the rest of the necessary rules in this regard. Anyone who comes under the framework of communism must take a solemn oath.

11. First, there must be a small establishment whose majority are altruists to the above-mentioned

extent. It means that they will work as diligently as contract-workers, ten to twelve hours a day and more. Each and every one will work according to his strength and receive according to his needs.

It will have all the forms of the government of a state. In this manner, even if the framework of this institution contains the entire world, and the brute-force government will be revoked completely, nothing will need to be changed in governance or work.

This institution will be like a global focal point with nations and states surrounding it to the farthest corners of the world. All who enter this framework of communism will have the same agenda and the same leadership as the center. They will be as one nation in profits, losses and results.

12. It is absolutely forbidden for any one from the institution to turn to any of the judicial establishments, etc., or any of the forms existing in the brute-force regime. All conflicts are to be resolved among themselves, meaning between the concerned parties. Public opinion, which condemns egoism, will condemn the guilty party for exploiting the righteousness of one's friend.

13. It is a fact that the Jews are hated by most nations, and are made fewer by them. It is true for the religious, the secular, and the communists. There is no tactic to fight against it except to bring true altruistic moral into the heart of the nations, to the point of cosmopolitism.

14. If one is forbidden to exploit one's friends, why should a nation be allowed to exploit its fellow

nations? What justifies one nation enjoying the land more than other nations? Therefore, international communism must be instituted.

As there are individuals who have been privileged by diligence, chance, or inheritance from ancestry to a greater share than the negligent, quite so is it among the nations. Hence, why should war on individuals be greater than against nations?

15. If you lived on an isle of savages that you could not bring to law and order except through religion, would you doubt it and let them destroy one another? Similarly, with regard to altruism, they are all savages, and there is no tactic they will accept unless through religion. Who would hesitate to abandon them to destroy each other with hydrogen bombs?

16. There are three bases to the expansion of faith: 1) Satisfaction of Desires; 2) Proofs; 3) and Propaganda.

  i. **Satisfaction of Desires** is like the perpetuating of the soul, reward, as well as national reward, which is the glorification of the nation.

  ii. **Proofs** is that the world cannot exist without it, much less in the days of the atom...

  iii. **Propaganda** can also be used instead of proof, if it is done with diligence.

17. Because of the craving for possessions, it is impossible to build Altruistic Communism unless Egoistic Communism comes first, as demonstrated by all the societies that wished to establish Altruistic

Communism prior to Marxism. However, now that a third of the world has already laid down their rudiments on an Egoistic Communist regime, it is possible to begin to establish a durable Altruistic Communism on a religious foundation.

18. Altruistic Communism will finally completely annul the brute-force regime. Instead, "every man will do that which is right in his own eyes." It should not surprise us, as it was unbelievable that children could be educated by explanation, but only through the cane. But today most people have accepted this and reduce the forceful rule on children.

This regards children who have neither patience nor knowledge. It is even more so with people, a collective of educated, knowledgeable people brought up to altruism. They will certainly not need the brute-force regime. Indeed, there is nothing more humiliating and degrading for a person than being under the brute-force government.

Even courthouses will not be necessary, unless some unusual event occurs, where the neighbors do not influence an exceptional individual. In that case, special pedagogues will be needed to turn that person around through argumentation and explanation of the benefit of society, until that person is brought back in line.

If one is stubborn, and it is all to no avail, then the public will turn away from that person as though from an outcast, until that person rejoins with the rules of society.

It turns out that after there is a settlement established on Altruistic Communism, with a majority of people who have actively taken these rules upon themselves, they will immediately decide not to bring each other to any court, governmental agency, or any other kind of force. Rather, everything will be done by gentle persuasion. Hence, no person is to be accepted into the society before he is tested to see if he is so crude that cannot be tutored into altruism.

19. It is important to make such a correction that no person will demand his needs from society. Instead, there will be selected people who will examine the needs of every person and provide for every single person. Public opinion will denounce one who claims something for oneself, such as today's thief and scoundrel.

   Thus, everyone's thoughts will be devoted to bestowal upon one's fellow person, as is the nature of any edification that calculates it, even before one feels one's own needs.

   If we want to jump on a table, we must prepare ourselves to jump much higher than the table, and then we will land on the table. However, if we want to jump only as high as the table, we will fall down.

20. Admittedly, the Egoistic Communism is but a step on the way to justice, a sort of "From *Lo Lishma* to *Lishma*" [from not-for-her-sake to for-her-sake]. But I say that the time for the second phase, namely Altruistic Communism, has arrived.

   First, it must be established in one country, as a model. After that the countries in the first phase will certainly accept it. Time is of the essence, since the shortcomings and brute-force used in Egoistic Communism deter the majority of the cultural world from this method altogether.

Thus, the world must be introduced to the perfect communism, and then most civilized countries in the world will undoubtedly accept it. It is of great concern that imperialism will abolish communism from the world, but if our perfect method will actually be publicized, imperialism will certainly be left as a king with no armies.

21. Clearly, no stable and proper social life is possible except when controversies among members of society are resolved by the majority. It therefore follows that there cannot be a good regime in a society unless the majority is good. A good society means that the majority in it is good, and a bad society means that the majority of it is bad. As I have said above, item 3, that communism must not be established before the majority of the people in society operate with a desire to bestow.

22. No circulation can secure a coercive rule over future generations, and neither public opinion nor education will help in this case, for they naturally tend to grow weaker. The exception is religion, which naturally grows stronger. We see from experience that nations that have accepted religion first coercively and compulsively, observe them willingly in the following generation. Moreover, they are dedicated and devoted to it.

We must understand that although the fathers took upon themselves Altruistic Communism because they were idealists, there is no guarantee that their children will follow them in this regime. Needless to say, if the fathers adopted communism by coercion, as is the manner in Egoistic Communism, it will not endure for generations, but will ultimately be overpowered and revoked. A regime cannot be imposed except through religion.

23. When I say that a communistic regime must not be instated before there is an altruistic majority, I do not mean that they will be willingly idealistic. Rather, it means that they will keep it for religious reasons, in addition to public opinion. This coercion is one that will last for generations, for religion is the primary compeller.

24. We must remember all the suffering, poverty, corruption and war, and the widows and orphans in the world, seeking salvation from the Altruistic Communism. At that time, it will not be difficult for one to dedicate one's entire life to save them from ruin and the dreadful pains. It is even more so with a young person, whose heart has not been stupefied by one's own shortcomings. That person will certainly support it with one's heart and soul.

THE NEGATIVE

1. If there is nationalization before the public is ready for it, meaning before each one has a sound basis, and secured cause for fuel to work, it is as though one ruins one's small house before he has the means to build another house.

2. Public equality does not mean equalizing the level of the talented and successful to the level of the negligent and oppressed. This would completely ruin the public. Rather, it means allowing each person in the public a middleclass standard of living. Thus, the negligent, too, will enjoy their lives as much the middleclass.

3. The freedom of the individual must be kept if it is not harmful to the majority of the public. The detrimental ones must not be pitied, and must be made harmless.

4. Current communism endures because of the idealists who lead it. They were idealists before they became communists. However, the second generation, when leaders are elected by the majority of the public, will gradually be repealed, assuming the form of Nazism or turning back to possessiveness. This is because nothing will stop them from exploiting other, negligent nations.

5. Egoistic Communism holds no war-preventing element, since the basis of all the wars is living territory, where each wants to build on the ruin of the other, whether justly, or because of envy that the other has more.

   Communism based on "mine is mine" in a framework of equal division does nothing to remove the envy of the nations with each other, much less the nations' lack of living space. It is also hopeless that the rich nations will give of their share to equalize with the poor because "mine is mine and yours is yours" does not necessitate it. Only communism of "mine is yours and yours is yours" will resolve it.

6. Even today we see that there is a global force that overpowered and conquered all the communist countries, behaving there as in its own home, just as it was in ancient history in Greece and Rome, etc. There is no doubt that this force will split into pieces in the future, and we already have Tito. When they split, they are certain to fight each other, for how does Russia govern Czechoslovakia, or the others, if not by the sword and the spear?

7. In communism, employers strive to diminish the consumption of the workers and increase their productivity. In imperialism, the employers want, and act to increase the consumption of the workers, and to equalize his productivity to consumption.

8. The rulers' and supervisors' class will ultimately create a sort of exile in Egypt over the working class since all the workers leave their surplus in the hands of the rulers, who take the greater part from them. Hence, they will not let a single worker get away from under their hands to another country. Thus, the workers will be caged, guarded like Israel in Pharaoh's Egypt.

9. The ruling class is destined finally to put all the old and handicapped in the working class to death, arguing that they eat more than they produce and they are parasites on the country. No one will die a natural death.

10. If communism spreads throughout the world, it will put to death every nation that eats more than it produces.

11. If the profiteers and the merchants become allotters, the buyers will become receivers of charity from the allotters, and the allotters will do with them as they see fit, or as much as they are afraid of the inspectors.

A Regime Cannot Exist on Spears Forever

12. Communism does not exist over an anti-communist society because a regime supported on bayonets and spears is unsustainable. Eventually, the majority in society will prevail and overthrow that government. Hence, an altruistic majority must be established first, and the government will be supported on will.

The Habit of Waves of Hatred and Envy Will Later Turn Against the Backward

13. Communism that is built on waves of hatred and envy will only succeed in overthrowing the bourgeois, not in benefiting the backward. On the contrary, the same ones that have grown accustomed to hatred and envy will turn the arrows of hatred against the backward once the bourgeois are gone.

Egoistic Communism Will Always Be at War with the Public

14. By its very nature, the communist regime will be compelled to always be at war with the anti-communists. This is because each person naturally

tends to be possessive. People naturally tend to take the cream and leave the meager whey for others.

Nature does not change by education or public opinion. It is unimaginable that one will ever willingly agree to just division, and army bayonets cannot turn nature around, much less education and public opinion.

Naturally-born idealists are few. If you should say that theft and robbery are well guarded in the capitalistic regime, I shall tell you that it is because the law permits legal competition. It is comparable to a person who gathers an association where the majority is murderers and robbers, and wants to rule over them and compel them to keep the law. But regarding the annulment of property, everyone is a robber.

Israel Is Qualified to Set an Example to All the Nations

15. Altruistic Communism is seldom found in the human spirit; hence, the nobler nation must take upon itself to set an example for the entire world.

The Country Is at Risk. Altruistic Communism Will Help With the Ingathering of the Exiles

16. The nation is at risk because each will flee to a different place before the economy is stabilized. This is because not every person can endure the test while there is a way to live comfortably.

In the Altruistic Communism the ideal will shine upon all people, giving them satisfaction that will make the suffering worthwhile. Moreover, it will draw the ingathering of the exiles from all the countries because the worries and survival wars everyone experiences overseas will motivate them to return to their land and live peacefully and justly.

The Philosophy Is Ready, Meaning Kabbalah Based on Religion

17. Each practical method also requires a renewed idealistic nourishment to contemplate, meaning a philosophy. As far as this is concerned, there is already a complete and ready-made philosophy, meaning Kabbalah, though it is intended only for the leaders.

Why Are We the Chosen People for It?

18. We must set a good example to the world because we are better qualified than all other nations. It is not because we are more idealistic than they are, but because we suffered from tyranny more than all other nations. For this reason, we are more prepared to seek counsel that will end tyranny from the land.

19. Ownership and control are not identical. For example, the owners of the railway are the shareholders, and the control is in the hands of the managers, though they have only a single share, or nothing at all. The same applies to the

shipping company, whose shareholders have no right to control or advise.

Take warships for example. They are owned by the state, yet no civilian is permitted aboard them. In addition, if the state should be in the hands of the proletariat by way of ownership, the management will ultimately be in the hands of the same managers as now, or others of likewise temper. The proletariat will have no greater foothold or benefit than they do now, unless the rulers are idealists, caring for the good of every single individual.

In a word, with respect to the government, it makes no difference whether the ownership is given to capitalists or to the state. In the end, it is the managers who will control them, not the owners. Hence, the correction of society should relate primarily to the executives. "The Taming of Power," 214 ["The Taming of Power" is a chapter in Bertrand Russell's (British Philosopher, 1872-1970) book, *Power*.]

And likewise, said Avniel in the Knesset (Herut, date...) [Benjamin Avniel (1906-1993), was an MK (member of Knesset, the Israeli Parliament) from the second elections to the sixth, and was part of the Herut party]. In Israel, the gap between the lowest functionary to the highest one is times 1.7. In England, it is times ten, and in the rest of the countries it is more or less the same. But in Russia it is times fifty. Thus, in a proletariat state the functionaries and the managers waste their energy much more than in capitalistic countries. This is because the government is oligarchic, and not democratic. In simple words, it is because the communists control anti-communists. There must be oligarchy. This will never change since communism means idealism, which is not in the majority.

20. Such a state, where the communists rule over anti-communists is obliged to be in the hands of a group of autocratic executives in absolute dictatorship. All the people in the country will be in their hands as though they are nothing. They must always keep the sword in their hands for killing, incarceration, concealed and revealed punishments, food depravation, and all sorts of punishments, according to each executive's arbitrary decision. All this is in order to keep the anti-communists in dreadful terror and fear, so they work for the state and not ruin it inadvertently or maliciously.

21. In such a state, the executives must make sure the citizens cannot choose a democratic management, since the majority of the country is anti-communistic.

22. In such a state, where the communists rule over the anti-communists, the managers must see that the citizens have no possibility for advertisement, or to disclose the dreadful injustice that is done to the people of the state or to the minorities in the state.

In other words, the printers are not to print and the administrators of the lecture halls must watch over the speakers so they do not criticize their deeds. They must punish harshly anyone who plans, or even thinks of criticizing their acts. Thus, the government will have full control to deal with them arbitrarily, and there will be no one to detain them. (*Power*, ... 21.)

23. Ethics cannot rely solely on education and pubic opinion, because public opinion necessitates only what is in the public's favor. Hence, if one comes and proves that morality is harmful to the public and vulgarity is more beneficial, they will immediately discard morality and choose vulgarity, as Hitler testifies.

24. The Egoistic Communism based on waves of envy and hate will never be rid of them. Rather, when there are no bourgeois, they will cast their hate on Israel. We must not be mistaken that communism will cure the loathing of Israel from the nations. Only Altruistic Communism can be expected to bring that remedy.

DEBATE

1. Clearly, the motto, "Each will receive according to his needs and work according to his ability," is absolute altruism. When this is applied, the majority of the public, or all of it, will be armed with the measure "mine is yours." Hence, do tell, which are the elements that can bring the public to this desire? Today's elements, namely the hatred of the capitalists and all sorts of animosities extending from it, will only bring one the opposite. It will instill the measure of "mine is mine and yours is yours" in people, which is Sodomite Rule, the opposite of love of man.

2. I have nothing to say to those who go with the flow, only with those who have their own mind and the strength to criticize.

3. Engels' fundamental concept, in the name of Marx, states, "The oppressed and exploited class cannot be liberated from the oppressing and exploiting class without also liberating the entire society from exploitation, oppression and class struggle once and for all."

    This is in contrast to contemporary communist conduct to slaughter and degenerate all the bourgeois parts of society. This powerful enmity will never be effaced from their children. It is also in contrast with the fact that they are establishing a sovereign, governing class, monitoring the working class. There is no more painful and regrettable class struggle than that. They pump out the fat from the workers' marrow and leave them the residue, along with perpetual fear of death, or of being sent to Siberia.

    Where is the salvation here? They have replaced the bourgeois class, which was not at all so terrible. In fact, its shadow has been lifted from them since the workers have the power to strike against them. They've substituted it with a sovereign class, governing and ruling a class of exploited slaves who are perpetually terrorized by a punishment far worse than they had in their war against the bourgeois.

4. The country is divided into two classes: the diligent, and the backward. The diligent are the employers and the leaders; the backward are the workers and the led. It is a natural law that the diligent will

exploit the backward. The only question is how much freedom, equality, and standard of living do they leave for the backward. Also, how much labor the diligent will demand of them?

The backward are always the vast majority in society. The diligent are but ten percent of it, which is the exact amount needed to operate society. If the percentage is increased or decreased, there is a crisis.

These are the crises in the bourgeois society. Crises in the communist society will take a different form, but with the same amount of pain. The name "diligent" also includes their heirs and those who bribe the diligent. The name "backward" relates also to diligent who for some reason have been thrown into the backward class.

5. Regarding religion: The permanent moral state does not stem from religion, but from science. "Empirio Criticism," 324 [This is a statement made by Lenin in his Book, *Materialism and Empirio Criticism*].

6. Morality based on public benefit exists in social animals, too. However, this is not enough since it changes to vulgarity where it is harmful to society, such as the great patriotic murderer, carried on the shoulders of the nationalists. Thus, only religion-based morality is durable, valid, and irreplaceable. We find the same among savage nations, whose level of morality is far greater than civilized nations.

7. A society cannot be good unless its majority is good. However, some stun or entice the evil

majority with all sorts of contrivances until they are compelled to choose a good leadership. This is what all democracies do. Alas, the majority finally learns, or others teach them, and they choose an evil leadership that matches their ill will.

8. We must understand why Marx and Engels decided that perfection of communism means "Working according the ability and receiving according to the needs." Who forced it upon them? Why was it not enough to receive according to one's production, and not to equalize one with a negligent, or with one without sons? The thing is that communism will not endure by way of egoism, but by the way of altruism, for the above-mentioned reasons.

NEWS

By the very same way they have exterminated the capitalists, they were also compelled to exterminate the farmers. In addition, in the sense of the joy of life, they will always be forced to destroy the proletariat. Although Marx and Engels were the first to place the correction of the world on the proletariat, it did not occur to them to do it coercively, but rather democratically. For this reason, the workers had to be the majority, and then establish a proletariat government where the leaders of the regime would gradually correct until they come to the abstract altruism – "each according to his actions, and each according to his needs."

Lenin added to it the establishment of the communist regime through forcing the minority opinion over the majority, hoping that afterwards, altruism would be conducted among them, too. All that was needed for this was an armed camp of proletariat. Since the property owners are scattered, the government could take it by force, and then come and defeat the weak and unorganized property owners.

In that, he disagreed with Marx and said that it is quite the contrary; in the backward countries it is easier to defeat them, as all that is needed was to turn the soldiers into communists and destroyers of the property owners, and to take their property. It is easier to incite soldiers to kill and loot the property owners in a backward country.

That is why he understood that he will not find a cruder multitude than in his own country, and therefore said that his country will be first. However, when he saw that in fact, it was not enough to destroy the capitalistic ten percent, but that millions of farmers must also be destroyed, he grew tired, because it is impossible to destroy half a nation.

Then came Stalin, who said that the end justifies the means, and took upon himself the task of destroying the farmers, too. He was successful.

However, not one of them also considered that in the end, they need the good will of the proletariat, so that they would work, and to instill the conduct of altruism in them, which would bring them to this motto. This is utterly impossible. Nature cannot be changed so that not only would one work for one's needs, but for his friend's needs. This is utterly impossible without coercion and enforcement. Ultimately, the majority will rise and revoke the regime.

Liars are those who say that idealism is either natural or a result of education. Rather, it is a direct result of religion. As long as religion did not sufficiently expand throughout the world, the entire world was barbaric, without an ounce of conscientiousness.

Only after servants of the Creator expanded, did the posterity of the agnostics become idealists. Thus, the idealist is only so because of his ancestry's commandment. However, it is an orphaned commandment, meaning without a commander.

If religion were to be cancelled altogether, all governments would then become Hitlers. Nothing would detain them from increasing the country's benefits incessantly. Even today, governments know no sentiments. However, there is still a limit to their acts between the still and the idealists in the country. When religion is revoked, it will not be difficult for rulers to uproot the remaining idealists, as it was not hard for Hitler and Stalin.

The difference between the idealist and religious is that the idealist's actions are baseless. He cannot convince anyone of his preference for justice, or who so necessitates it. Perhaps it is but faintness of heart, as Nietzsche said? He will not have a single sensible word to utter, which is why Hitler and Stalin overpowered them. However, the religious will boldly counter that it is so commanded by the Lord, and would give his life for it...

If my words yield benefit, good. If not, the last generations will know why communism was revoked, that it was not because it could not be sustained, as capitalists say, but because the leaders did not understand how to establish that regime. They erected a regime of egoism where they should have established a regime of altruism.

If anyone should disagree with me and say that education will suffice for that, I permit him to establish for himself a society based solely on education, but I will not partake in it. I know all too well that these are idle things. Thus, might he assist me in establishing a religion-based society?

Appendices and Drafts

[Fourteen pieces that form appendices or drafts to the essay presented in Part One]

SECTION ONE

[This section contains inscriptions that appear to be headlines that the author wrote for his own needs toward writing the essay presented in Part One. It is a kind of first, and general draft.]

"Critical communism has never refused, or refuses now, to welcome the abundance of ideological, ethical, psychological, and educational ideas that may be reached by studying the various forms of communism" (Antonio Labriola (1843-1904), an Italian Marxist theoretician).[1]

2. "Were we to wish to think today as Marx and Engels did, at a time when if they themselves were here today, they would be thinking otherwise ... defending the dead letter of the latter," etc. (from Georgi Plekhanov' introductions to the *Communist Manifesto*).[2]

---

[1]   Antonio Labriola, *Essays on the Materialist Conception of History*, Part 1: "In Memory of the Communist Manifesto," url: http://www.marxists.org/archive/labriola/works/al00.htm#

[2]   Georgi Plekhanov, "The Initial Phases of the Theory of the Class Struggle: An Introduction to the Second Russian Edition of the *Manifesto of the Communist Party*," url: https://www.marxists.org/archive/plekhanov/1898/initial-phases.htm

The Positive

1. Evidence for the altruistic communism.
2. For the rules of the altruistic communist society.
3. For the international communism.
4. For a beneficial religion.
5. Promoting the expansion of the religion.
6. Egoistic communism precedes the altruistic communism.
7. For the keeping of Judaism.

The Negative

1. The weakness of the regime of egoistic communism (8).
2. Wars will not become obsolete (9).
3. Proof that egoistic communism cannot last (10).
4. Motives from Zionism (11).
5. Israel must be a role model for the nations (12).
6. Concerning the egoistic regime (13).
7. Ethics (14).

10/2 14/8 14/4 Communism is egoistic along the way, although eventually it is altruistic.

8/1 3/3 The world should be divided into two kinds: egoists and altruists 0/0.

10/3 10/1 10/2 10/6 The majority of the public is always anti-communistic.

8/2 For this reason, the communist regime must rely on bayonets.

13/7 The drawbacks in the egoistic communism governance.

From 8/9 to 9/1 Communism will not save us from wars.

Communism must be international, from 3/2 to 12/1/2.

11/1 Strengthening Zionism, especially the kibbutzim, which are in danger of being cancelled.

A communistic rule over anti-communists will not survive on bayonets. Those idealists who are in power today will not be elected in the second generation, but rather egoistic managers, like them, and they will turn into Nazism.

I am speaking only of the proletariat, the weak, and of those idealists who dedicate their lives for them. I do not, however, speak of the diligent because they will not be deficient under any regime. Even in the worst regime, they will not be deprived, and it makes no difference whether they are called "industrialists," "merchants," or "managers," "supervisors" or "distributors."

Still, although the coupling of altruists with egoists had so succeeded as to overthrow the bourgeois government, it is utterly unfit to establish a happy cooperative society, as the founders wish. Moreover, it is to the contrary, since that coupling of the idealistic communists with the oppressed egoists is bound to break up, leaving social chaos in its wake.

1) How much to leave.

2) What is the measure of enslavement.

3) What is the measure of freedom.

There is no correction to the weak unless they choose the committee.

3) The diligent will not let them out of their countries.

3) In the end, they will put to death the elderly and the sick.

1) When traders become distributors, the buyers will become receivers of charity.

2) Ownership and control are not the same.

3) In a compulsory regime there will not be democratic elections.

2) In such a regime, the citizens are completely inconsequential in the eyes of the government.

2) In such a regime the managers will enslave even more.

2) In such a regime the employers will be able to conceal their cruelty.

Explaining Hitlerism

1) Religion is the only sound basis for corrections

1) Religion is the only sound basis for raising the moral standard

1) Even if it begins with coercion, it ends in willingness

2) Communism must not be established before altruism has spread through the majority of the public

1) Religion and ideals complement one another: one is for the few, the other is for the masses.

3) Due to man's craving to work less and receive more, they will be able to assume a communistic religion before an egoistic religion has encompassed a third of the world.

4) If you came to an island where savages destroy one another, would you hesitate to offer them a religion by which to save their lives?

5) Man will not be able to settle for dry commandments; he needs a philosophy that will explain to him his good deeds. This is what they have prepared.

SECTION TWO

For the Introduction

1. I have already conveyed the rudiments of my perception in 1933. I have also spoken to the leaders of the generation, but at the time, my words were not accepted, though I was screaming like a crane, warning about the destruction of the world. Alas, it made no impression.

   Now, however, after the atom and hydrogen bombs, I think the world will believe me that the end of the world is coming rapidly, and Israel will be the first nation to be burned, as in the previous war. Thus, today it is good to awaken the world to accept the only remedy, and they will live and exist.

2. We must understand why Marx and Engels necessitated the ultimate communism, where each works according to his ability and receives according to his needs. Why do we need this strict condition, being the measure of "mine is yours and yours is yours," the absolute altruism?

   In that regard, I have come to prove in this article that there is no hope for communism to exist, if it is not brought to this end, which is complete altruism. Until then, it is nothing but phases in communism.

Once I have proven the rightness of the motto, "Each according to his ability, and each according to his needs," we must see if these phases can yield this outcome.

Today, the definitions, "bourgeois" and "proletariat," no longer suffice to explain the history of economy. Rather, we need more general terms: the "Diligent Class" and the "Backward Class" (above in the section "Debate," item 4).

After twenty-five years of experience, we are baffled regarding the complete happiness that the communist regime had promised us. Its opponents say it is the absolute evil, and its supporters say that it is heaven on earth.

Indeed, we must not cast off the words of the opponents at a stroke, because when one wants to know another's properties, he must ask both his friends and his foes. It is a rule that the friends know only the virtues and not a single flaw, for "love covers all transgressions." The foes are the opposite: They know only the faults, for "hate covers all virtues."

Thus, one knows the truth when hearing the words of both. I wish to examine communism thoroughly, and explain its advantages and disadvantages. Mostly, I wish to explain the corrections, how all its shortcomings can be corrected so that everyone will see and admit that this regime is indeed the regime that brings both justice and happiness.

How happy we were when communism came to practical experimentation in a nation as big as Russia. It was clear to us that after a few years

56

the government of justice and happiness would appear before the entire world, and thus the capitalist government would vanish from the world in a wink of an eye.

Yet, that was not the case. Quite the contrary, all the civilized nations speak of the Soviet communist regime as of a bad deformity. Hence, not only was the bourgeois regime not cancelled, it rather grew twice as strong as before the Soviet experiment.

SECTION THREE

Why did communism had to have taken the form of "each according to his ability, and each according to his actions"? A communist government cannot endure over an anti-communist society, since a government supported on bayonets is unsustainable.

Communism built on waves of envy can only overthrow and ruin the bourgeois, but not benefit the backward proletariat. Conversely, when the bourgeois are annihilated, the arrows of odium will aim at the backward.

Nothing can guarantee a powerful government over the future generations except religion. Even if the progenitors are idealists, and have assumed the communism, there is no certainty that their progeny would pursue it. All the more so, if the progenitors had assumed it by force and coercion, which is the conduct in egoistic communism, they will ultimately rise and demolish it.

A communist regime cannot exist atop an anti-communist society. It would have to fight the anti-communists throughout its days. This is because every person is naturally possessive; one cannot work without motivation.

The army's bayonets will not turn man's nature around, and the idealists are few. Several thousand years of penalties rest on the heads of the thieves, the robbers, and the fraudulent, yet they have not changed their nature even though they can obtain everything legally.

It is much the same as one coming upon a society of thieves and murderers, wanting to lead them and restrict them to legal ways by force. It must explode.

Double. Double. Double.

Because the majority opinion is guaranteed to win, it is all the more so with the implementation of communism. It will not persist but through the majority of the public. Hence, we must perpetuate the moral level of the majority of the public in such a way that it will never be corrupted.

Religion is the only sound basis that will persist for generations. Communism must be transformed to the mode of "mine is yours and yours is yours," meaning absolute altruism. After the majority of the public achieves it, it will observe, "Each will work according to his ability and receive according to his needs."

Before the majority of the public achieves this level of morality, it is forbidden to nationalize the property for the above-mentioned reasons.

SECTION FOUR

Nationalization before the public is ready, for it is similar to wrecking one's rickety house before one has the means to build a strong one.

Just division does not mean equalizing the diligent to the backward. This would be ruinous to the public. Rather, it means equalizing the backward to the diligent.

Egoistic Communism exists now through a group of idealists that lead it. Yet, in future generations, the public will not elect idealists, but only the most capable, who are not limited by the ideal, and then communism will take on the form of Nazism.

In the Egoistic Communism, the employers wish to reduce the consumption of the worker and increase the produce, which will always be questionable if sufficient. Imperialism is better than that, since the employers want to increase the consumption of the worker and equalize the productivity to the consumption.

SECTION FIVE

The definitions, "bourgeois" and "proletariat," are no longer sufficient to explain history. Instead, it should be divided into "Diligent Class" and "Backward Class."

It is a natural law that the diligent class will exploit the backward class, like fish at sea, where the strong swallow the weak. It makes no difference if the diligent are bourgeois, or the functionaries of the communistic government. Rather, the question is how much freedom and enjoyment do they leave for the backward.

The diligent class is ten percent, and the backward class led by them is ninety percent of society. There is no correction for the backward unless they themselves choose those diligent that will govern them. If they do not have this power, they will end up being uninhibitedly exploited by the diligent.

SECTION SIX

The diligent class, meaning the rulers and the inspectors, are bound to create an exile such as in Egypt over the backward class, who are the workers. This is because the rulers accumulate all the surplus of the workers in their hands and take the lion's share.

In addition, for purposes of the benefit of the public, they will not let any worker escape from under their hands to a different country; they will guard them like Israel in Egypt. No slave shall leave them and be free. Ultimately, the diligent class will put to death all the elderly and handicapped who eat and do not work, or even if they eat more than they can work, as it is detrimental to society, as it is known that they have no sentiments.

When merchants and brokers become allotters, the buyers will become recipients of charity from their hands. Their fate would be determined by the mercy of the allotters, or as much as they fear the inspectors, should they take interest in that.

Since ownership and control are not the same, for example, with a ship that belongs to the state, every citizen has ownership over it, yet no right of entry, but only as the administration that controls it sees fit. Also, even if there is a proletariat government, they will have no preference in government properties than they have now in the bourgeois property. This is because all the control will be held by the executives alone, which are today's bourgeois, or those like them.

Such a state, where communists govern anti-communists, must be in the hands of oligarchy, in complete dictatorship, where all the citizens are regarded as nothing, subject to brutal punishment according to the arbitrary heart of each and every executive. Otherwise, they will not secure the sustenance of the needs of the state. In such a regime, the government must ensure that there are no democratic elections since the majority of the public are anti-communists.

Egoistic Communism does not liberate the proletariat whatsoever. On the contrary, instead of bourgeois employers, who are lenient with the workers, they will institute a class of executives and supervisors who will enslave the proletariat by coercion and harsh and bitter punishments. The oppression and the exploitation will be doubled, and it will not be easier on them in any way if the exploitation is for the good of the country, because in the end, the employers and the oppressors take the cream, and the workers get the meager whey. In return, they are placed under constant fear of death, or punishment harsher than death.

In such a state, where communists rule over anti-communists, the executives must see that the citizens cannot discover the burden and oppression they are under. Thus, after all the works are in their hands, they will forbid the printers from printing, and the speakers from speaking, so they do not criticize their deeds whatsoever. Instead, they will be compelled to lie and cover up for them, and depict a heaven on earth, and their plight will never become known.

It will be even more so with minorities who are not favored by the executives for whatever reason. They will be able to annihilate them without shame or fear that it will become known outside. And what will become of the Jews, whom the majority of the world hates?

Indeed, it is the absolute truth that there cannot be a good and complete society unless its majority is good because the management depicts the quality of society, and the society is elected by the majority. If the majority is bad, the management will necessarily be bad, as well, for the wicked will not place over them rulers of whom they do not approve.

We need not deduce from the modern democracies, as they use various tactics to deceive the constituency. When they grow wiser and understand their cunningness, the majority will certainly elect a management according to their spirit. And their main tactic is that they first sanctify people with good reputation and promote them either as wise or as righteous, and then the masses believe and elect them. But a lie does not persist forever.

This explains Hitlerism. What happened to the Germans is one of nature's wonders. They were considered among the most civilized nations, and all of a sudden, overnight, they became savages, worse than even the most primitive nations in history.

Moreover, Hitler was elected by the majority's vote. In light of the above, it is very simple: Indeed, the majority of the public, which is essentially evil, possesses no opinions, even among the most civilized nations. Rather, they deceive the majority of the public. Hence, even though the majority of the public is evil, there can be a good leadership.

However, should an evil person, capable of uncovering the deceit that the managers employ with the famous people they create, come and present the people that should be elected according to their spirit and desire, as did Hitler (and Lenin and Trotsky [Leon Trotsky, 1879-1940, a Jewish Marxist revolutionary]), it is no wonder that they overthrow the fraudulent and elect evil leaders according to their spirit.

Thus, Hitler was indeed elected democratically, and the majority of the public united behind him. Afterward, he subdued and uprooted all the idealistic people, and did with nations as he wished, and as the people wished.

This is the whole novelty. Since the dawn of time, it has never happened that the majority of the public governed a state. Either the autocrats did, who, at the end of the day, do have some measure of morality, or the oligarchy, or the deceitful democrats. The majority of the simple folk ruled only in the days of Hitler, who, in addition, promoted turpitude toward other nations. He elevated public benefit to the level of devotion since he understood the frame of mind of sadists. When given room to discharge their sadism, they would pay for it with the lives.

SECTION SEVEN

Egoistic Communism cannot prevent wars, since the diligent nations, or the ones rich in raw materials, will not want to share equally with the poor and backward nations. Hence, once again we must not hope for peace, except by means of the prevention of wars, meaning by preparing arms to guard against the envy and odium of the poor and backward nations, just as today. Even more so, there will be even more wars due to changes in ideals, such as Titoism and Zionism.

I have already spoken and wrote about it in 1933, and I have screamed as a crane that today's wars will destroy the world, but they did not believe it. But now, after the atom and hydrogen bombs, I think that everyone will believe me that if we are not saved from wars, it will be the end of the world.

SECTION EIGHT

If communism is just toward each nation, then it is just toward all the nations. What prerogative and ownership over raw materials in the soil has one nation over others? Who legislated this proprietary law? All the more so when they have acquired it by means of swords and bayonets!

Also, why should one nation exploit another if it is unjust to every individual? In a word: As abolition of property is just for the individual, so it is just for every nation. Only then will there be peace on earth.

Consider this: If proprietary laws and rules of inheritance do not permit possession rights to individuals, why would they permit an entire nation? As just division is applied among individuals within the nation, there should also be internationally just division in raw materials, productive means, and accumulated properties for all the nations equally. There should be no difference between white and black, civilized and primitive, just as among individuals within a single nation. There should be no division whatsoever among individuals, a single nation, or all the nations in the world. While there is any differentiation, wars will not end.

There is no hope of reaching International Communism through Egoistic Communism. Even if America, India, and China should adopt a communistic regime, there is still no element that will compel Americans to equalize their standard of living with the savage and primitive Africans and Indians.

All the cures of Marx and Lenin will be to no avail here, inciting the poor class to rob the wealthy class, since the wealthy have already made arms to guard themselves. Thus, if it is to no avail, then the entire Egoistic Communism was in vain, for it will not prevent wars whatsoever.

SECTION NINE

It is a fact that Israel is hated by all the nations, whether for religious, racial, capitalist, communist, or for cosmopolitan reasons, etc. It is so because the hatred precedes all reasons, but each merely resolves its loathing according to its own psychology. No counsel will help here, except to initiate international, moral, and Altruistic Communism among all nations.

Israel must be the first among the nations to assume the international, Altruistic Communism. It must be a model demonstrating the good and beauty of this government. Because they suffer and will suffer from the tyranny of the nations more than all other nations, they are like the heart that burns before all the other organs. Hence, they are better suited to adopt the proper government first.

Our very existence in the state of Israel is in danger since according to the present economic order, it will take a long time before our economy is stabilized. Very few will be able to endure the experience of the ordeal in our country while they can immigrate to other, wealthy countries. Bit-by-bit, they will escape the discomfort until too few remain to merit the name "State," and they will be swallowed among the Arabs.

But if they accept the International Altruistic Communist regime, not only will they have the satisfaction of being the avant-garde for the delivery of the world, for which they will know that it is worth the suffering, but they will also be able to control their souls and lower the standard of living when needed. They will be able to work hard enough to secure a solid economy for the state.

It is even more so with kibbutzim, whose very existence is built on idealism, which will naturally wane in future generations, as ideals are not hereditary. Undoubtedly, they will be the first to ruin.

SECTION TEN

Religion is the only sound basis to raise the moral level of society until each person works according to his ability and receives according to his needs.

Unclear...

If you lived on an isle of savages, whose lives you could not save, preventing them from ferociously exterminating themselves, except by means of religion, would you then doubt ordering their lives with a religion that would suffice to save this nation from eradication from the world?

With respect to Altruistic Communism, everyone is savage. There is no ploy to impose such a regime on the world, except by means of religion, for religious compulsion becomes agreeable in the progeny, as we have seen happen in nations that have accepted religion by force and coercion.

However, in coercion through education and public opinion, which is not hereditary in the progeny, it only diminishes in time. Hence, would you say that it is better that the entire world destroys each other than to impose on them a certain cause to lead them to life and happiness? It is hard to believe that any sane person would hesitate here.

It is impossible to have a stable democratic society except by means of a society whose majority is good and honest, since society is led by the majority, for better or for worse. Hence, the Altruistic Communist regime must not be established unless the majority of the public is ready to commit to it for generations. That can only be secured through religion because the nature of religion is that even though it begins coercively, it ends voluntarily.

Religion and idealism complement each other. Where the ideal cannot be in the majority, religion forcefully rules the primitive majority, incapable of ideals due to its possessiveness and its desire to work less than his friend and receive more.

It is impossible to erect the Altruistic Communism before the Egoistic Communism expands. However, now that a third of the world has assumed the Egoistic Communism, the power of religion can be used to establish Altruistic Communism.

Humankind will not suffice with dry decrees without accompanying them with reasonable explanations that support and strengthen these conducts, meaning a philosophic method. In that regard, there is already an entire philosophy concerning the will to bestow, which is the Altruistic Communism, sufficient to contemplate for one's entire life, and thus strengthen oneself through acts of bestowal.

SECTION ELEVEN

Egoistic Communism will ultimately adopt the form of pure Nazism, but in the appearance of National Communism. However, this difference of names does not inhibit anyone from the satanic acts of Hitler. Thus, the Russians will be the "Master Nation," and the entire world their submissive servants as in Hitler's way.

In the bourgeois regime, free competition is the primary fuel for success. The industrialists and the merchants play in it; the winners are very happy, and those who do not win suffer a bitter end. In between them is the proletariat, having no share in this game. It is seemingly neutral, neither rising nor falling. However, because of its ability to strike, its standard of living is secured.

Ultimately, in both the communist and the bourgeois governments, the backward are unfit for leadership, although they are the majority of the public. Rather, they must elect leaders from among the diligent. However, because they are elected by them, they can be hopeful of not being exploited so much.

Conversely, in the Egoistic Communist government, the managers are not elected by the majority of the public, since they are anti-communists, as in Russia and the others, where the elected are only from among the communists. Hence, they face a bitter end indeed, since the proletariat does not have a single representative in the leadership.

All the above adheres to the rule that the proletariat are anti-communists by nature. The proletariats are not idealists; they are the backward majority of society, and think that "just division" means that they receive an equal share with the diligent. The diligent will never want that.

My words relate only to the proletariat, meaning to the backward, who are the majority of society. The diligent and the intellectuals will always suck the cream, either in a communist government, or in a bourgeois government. It is reasonable to think that many of them will be better off in a communist regime, since they will not fear criticism, as it is written in item...

Only you, the backward proletariat, will be the worst off in a communist regime. However, the diligent class will have a different name: managers and supervisors. They will be better off because they will be rid of the competition, which takes its toll on the bourgeois, and will receive their share persistently and abundantly.

The backward have no counsel and contrivance to terminate the fear, unemployment, and ignominy, except for Altruistic Communism. Hence, my words are not aimed at the diligent and the intellectuals, as they will certainly not accept my words, but only at the proletariat and the backward. They will be able to understand me, and to them I speak, as well as to those who spare the lives of the backward and sympathize with their anguish.

It is one of man's freedoms not to be tied to one place, like plants, which cannot leave their habitat. Hence, each country must ensure that it does not inhibit citizens from moving to another country. It must also be ensured that no country closes its gates before strangers and immigrants.

A government of Altruistic Communism must not be instigated before the majority of the public is prepared for bestowal upon one another.

Ultimately, Altruistic Communism will encircle the entire world, and the entire world will have the same standard of living. However, the actual process is slow and gradual. Each nation, whose majority of the public has been educated to bestowal upon one another, will enter the International Communistic framework first.

All the nations that have already entered the International Communistic framework will have an equal standard of living. Thus, the surplus of a rich or diligent nation will improve the standard of living of a backward or poor nation in raw materials and productive means.

The religious form of all the nations should first obligate its members to bestowal upon each other to the extent that (the life of one's friend will come before one's own life), as in "Love thy friend as thyself." One will not take pleasure in society more than a backward friend.

This will be the collective religion of all the nations that will come within the framework of communism. However, besides that, each nation may follow its own religion and tradition, and one must not interfere in the other.

The rules of the equal religion for the entire world are as follows:

1. One should work for the well-being of people as much as one can and even more than one's ability, if needed, until there is no hunger or thirst in the entire world.

2. One may be diligent, but no person shall enjoy the society more than the backward. There will be an equal standard of living for all.

3. Though there is religion, tokens of due honors should be imparted according to the religion; the greater the benefit one contributes to society, the higher the decoration one shall receive.

4. Refraining from showing one's diligence toward the benefit of society will induce punishment according to the laws of society.

5. Each and every one is committed to the labor of raising ever higher the living standard of the world society, so all the people in the world will

enjoy their lives and will feel more and more happiness.

6. The same applies for spirituality, though not everyone is obligated to engage in spirituality, but only special people, depending on the need.

7. There will be a sort of high-court. Those who will want to dedicate their labor for spiritual life will have to be permitted to do so by this court.

Elaborating on the other necessary laws:

Anyone, individual, or a group, who comes under the framework of the Altruistic Communism, must take a solemn oath to keep all that because the Lord has so commanded. At the very least one must pledge to teach one's children that the Lord has so commanded.

Those who say that the ideal is enough for them should be accepted and tested. If it is so, they may be accepted. However, they must still promise not to pass their heretical ways to their children, but hand them over to be educated by the state. If one accepts neither, he should not be accepted whatsoever. He would corrupt his friends and he would lose more than he would gain.

First, there must be a small establishment, whose majority of the public is willing to work as much as it can and receive as much as it needs for religious reasons. It will work as diligently as contract-workers, even more than the eight-hour workday. It will contain all the forms of government of a complete state. In a word, the order of that small society will be sufficient for all the nations in the world, without adding or subtracting.

This institution will be like a global focal point for nations and states surrounding it to the farthest corners of the world. All who enter this framework shall assume the same leadership and the same agenda as the institution. Thus, the entire world will be a single nation, in profits, losses, and results.

Judgments relying on force will be completely revoked in this institution. Rather, all conflicts among the members of society shall be resolved among the concerned parties. General public opinion shall condemn anyone who exploits the righteousness of his friend for his own good.

There will still be a courthouse, but it will only serve to sort out doubts that will come between people, but it will not rely on any force. One who rejects the court's decision will be condemned by public opinion, and that is all.

We should not doubt its sufficiency, as it was unbelievable that children could be educated only by explanation, but only through the cane. However, today, the greater part of civilization has taken upon itself to refrain from beating children, and this upbringing is more successful than the previous method.

If there is one who is exceptional in society, he must not be brought before a court relying on force, but must be reformed through argumentation and explanation. If all the counsels are to no avail, the public will turn away from that person as though from an outcast. Thus, he will not be able to corrupt others in society.

It is important to make such a correction that no person will demand his needs from society. Instead, there will be appointees who will go from door to door, examining the needs of every one, and they will provide for him by themselves. Thus, everyone's thoughts will be devoted to bestowal upon one's fellow person, and he will never have to think of his own needs.

It is based on the observation that in consumption we are like any other animal. In addition, every loathsome act in the world stems from consumption. Conversely, we see that every joyous deed in the world comes from the attribute of bestowal upon one's fellow person. Thus, we should scrimp and reject thoughts of consumption for self, and fill our minds only with thoughts of bestowal upon our fellow person. This is possible in the above manner.

The freedom of the individual must be kept as long as it is not harmful to society. However, one who wishes to leave the society in favor of another must not be detained in any way, even if it is harmful to society, and even that, in a way that the society is not ruined altogether.

SECTION TWELVE

Circulation

There are three rudiments to the expansion of religion: Satisfaction of Desires, Proof, and Circulation.

1. Satisfaction of Desires:

   In every person, even secular, there is an unknown spark that demands unification with God. When it sometimes awakens, it awakens a passion to know God, or deny God, which is the same. If someone generates the satisfaction of this desire in that person, he will agree to anything. To that we must add the matter of the immortality of the soul, the reward in the next world, glory of the individual, the glory of the nation.

2. Proof:

   There is no existence to the world without it, all the more so in the days of the atom and the hydrogen bombs.

3. Circulation:

   People must be hired to circulate the above words in the public.

Egoistic Communism precedes the Altruistic Communism, for once it has control so as to abolish property, it is possible to educate that the annulment of property will be due to love of others.

The second phase of communism, being Altruistic Communism, must be hurried, since the shortcomings and force used in Egoistic Communism, deter the world from this method altogether. Hence, it is time to uncover the final stage of Altruistic Communism, which possesses all the pleasantness, and has no blemish.

We must also fear, lest the third war breaks out first, and communism will vanish from the world. In a word, there is no harder blow to the capitalist government than this above-mentioned perfect form of communism.

We are already witnessing that the capitalistic regime is strong and the proletariat of the capitalistic countries loathe the communist regime. This is happening because of the coercion and the force necessitated in it because of the control of a small group of communists over an anti-communist society.

Hence, we are not to expect that the regime will be cancelled by itself. Quite the contrary, time works in their favor. As long as communistic governments surround the world, the coercion and subjection entailed in it will be revealed, which every ordinary person utterly loathes, since one will sacrifice everything for one's freedom.

There is another thing: Since communism is not spreading in civilized countries, but in primitive ones, eventually there will be a society of rich countries with high living standard and capitalistic government, and a society of poor countries with a low standard of living and a communist government. That will be the end of communism. Not a single free person will want to hear of it; it will be abhorred as the concept of slaves sold for life is abhorred today.

For expansion and circulation: We must remember that all the agony, poverty and slaying, etc., cannot be corrected except through Altruistic Communism. In that event, it will not be hard for a person to give his life for it.

Judaism must present something new to the nations. This is what they expect from the return of Israel to the land! It is not in other teachings, for in that we never innovated. In them, we have always been their disciples. Rather, it is the wisdom of religion, justice, and peace. In this, most nations are our disciples, and this wisdom is attributed to us alone.

If this return is cancelled, Zionism will be cancelled altogether. This country is very poor, and its residents are destined to endure much suffering. Undoubtedly, either they or their children will gradually leave the country, and only an insignificant number will remain, which will ultimately be swallowed among the Arabs.

The solution for it is only Altruistic Communism. Not only does it unite all the nations to be as one, helping one another, it also endows each with tolerance to one another. Most importantly: Communism produces great power to work; hence, the labor productivity will compensate for the disadvantages of poverty.

If they assume this religion, the Temple can be built and the ancient glory restored. This would certainly prove to the nations the rightness of Israel's return to their land, even to the Arabs. However, a secular return such as today's does not impress the nations whatsoever, and we must fear lest they will sell Israel's independence for their needs, needless to mention returning Jerusalem. This would even frighten the Catholics.

SECTION THIRTEEN

Thus far, I have shown that communism and altruism are one and the same, and also, that egoism and anti-communism are the same. However, all this is my own doctrine. If you ask the communist leaders themselves, they will deny it unreservedly.

Instead, they would maintain that they are far from any sentimentality and bourgeois morality, and seek only justice by way of "mine is mine and yours is yours." (All this has come to them because of their connection with the proletariat.) Thus, let us examine things according to their perception, and scrutinize this justice that they seek.

According to the development of today's governments, the definitions "bourgeois" and "proletariat" are no longer sufficient to explain history. We need more general definitions. They should be determined by the names "diligent" (which in the second regime are the capitalist, and in the communistic regime), and "backward."

Any society is divided into diligent and backward. Some twenty percent are diligent, and eighty percent are backward. It is a natural law that the diligent class exploits the backward class, like fish at sea, where the strong swallow the weak. In that regard, it makes no difference whether the diligent are bourgeois capitalists, or managers, supervisors, or intellectuals. In the end, the same diligent twenty percent will always suck the cream and leave the meager whey to the backward. But the question is how much they exploit the backward, and which kind exploit the backward more—the bourgeois, or the managers and supervisors.

SECTION FOURTEEN

The basis of this entire explanation is the manifestation of the substance of creation, spiritual and corporeal, being nothing but the will to receive, which is existence from absence. However, what this substance receives extends existence from existence.

Thus, it is clearly known what is good and what the Lord demands of us, namely, equivalence of form. By the nature of its creation, our body is but a desire to receive, and not to bestow at all. This is opposite to the Creator, who is all to bestow, and not to receive at all, because from whom would He receive? It is in this disparity of form that creation has become separated from the Creator.

Hence, we are commanded to deeds in Torah and *Mitzvot* (precepts) that bring contentment to the maker, and to bestow upon one's fellow person. This is in order to acquire the form of bestowal and cleave once more to the Creator as before creation.

THE DIFFERENCES BETWEEN ME AND SCHOPENHAUER

[Arthur Schopenhauer (1788-1860), German philosopher]

1. He perceives it as an essence on its own, while I perceive it as a type and a predicate. Its essence may be unknown, but whatever it may be, it extends existence from existence.

2. He perceives the desire itself as an ambition that no goal can end, but is rather a constant ascent and perpetual drive. With me, however, it is limited to receiving certain things, and can be satiated, meaning directed.

   However, attaining the goal increases the will to receive, as in, he who has one hundred wants two hundred. Prior to that, the will to receive was limited to obtaining only one hundred; it did not want two hundred. In this manner, the perpetual desire is expansion of the desire; it is the will to receive itself.

3. He does not differentiate between the will to bestow and the will to receive. With me, only the will to receive is the essence of the creature, while the will to bestow in it is a Godly Light, ascribed to the Creator, not to the creature.

4. He perceives the desire itself as an object, considering it a form and an occurrence in the object. With me, the emphasis is rather on the form of the desire, meaning the will to receive, but the carrier of the form of the will to receive is an unknown essence.

1) ...Since he considers the desire the subject, he must define some general, formless desire. Thus, he chooses the endless aspiration for materials, and what it wants is the form. Yet, in truth, there is no endless yearning here, but a growing desire that grows according to the direction, and it is a form and a case in the desire.

A. In his method, it is an essence; in mine, a form.

B. In his method it is a never-ending desire; in mine, it is limited in its direction.

C. In his method, there is no difference between bestowing and receiving; in mine, the will to bestow is a spark of the Creator.

D. In his method, the yearning is a substance, and the quality of the reception, the form; in mine, the quality of reception is the substance of creation and the subject of the quality is unknown. Whatever it is, it is existence from existence.

Part Two

LEADERS OF THE GENERATION

The masses tend to believe that the leader has no personal commitments and interests, but that he has dedicated and abandoned his private life for the common good. Indeed, this is how it should be. If the leader harms a member of the public due to personal interest, he is a traitor and a liar. Once the public learns of it, they will immediately trample him to the ground.

There are two kinds of personal interests: 1) Material interests; 2) Mental interests. There is not a leader in the world who will not fail the public for mental interests. For example, if one is merciful, and hence refrains from uprooting evildoers or warning about them, then he ruins the public in favor of a personal interest. He might also be afraid of vengeance, even the vengeance of the Creator, and thus deter from making necessary corrections.

Thus, if he wishes to annul material interests, he will not wish to annul the idealistic or religious interests in favor of the public, though they may be only his own personal sensations. The general public may have no dealings with them, for they notice only the word "interest," since even the most idealistic thing does not stand in the way of "interest."

ACTION BEFORE THOUGHT

As in desire and love, the exertion over an object creates love and appreciation toward the object. In much the same way, good deeds beget love for the Creator, love begets adhesion, and adhesion begets intelligence and knowledge.

THREE POSTULATES [AXIOMS]

Seemingly free, seemingly immortal, seemingly existing [the last word is unclear in the manuscript and is therefore a speculation]. They are relative to the practical reason (ethics), to the most sublime good.

TRUTH AND FALSEHOOD

It is known that thought, matter, and desire are two modifications [differences of form] of the same thing. Thus, the psychological replica of physical absence and existence is truth and falsehood. In this manner, truth, like existence, is the thesis, and falsehood, like absence, is the antithesis. The desired synthesis is the progeny of both.

[new page]

[Here, and below, the words, "new page," mark the beginning of a new page or a new section in the manuscript.]

PERSONAL OPINION AND PUBLIC OPINION

The opinion of the individual is like a mirror where all the pictures of the beneficial and detrimental acts are gathered. One looks at those experiences, sorts out the good and beneficial ones, and rejects the acts that have harmed him. This is called the "memory brain."

For example, the merchant follows in his mind all kinds of merchandise where he suffered losses, and why. It is likewise with merchandise that profited him, and the reasons. They are arranged like a mirror of experiences in his mind. Subsequently, he sorts out the good, and rejects the bad. Finally, he becomes a good and successful merchant. One deals in much the same way with every experience in life.

In much the same way, the public has a collective mind, a Memory Brain, and collective imagination, where all the acts related to the general public are imprinted with regard to every person, the beneficial ones and the detrimental ones. And they also choose the beneficial acts and doers, and want those who do them to persist. In addition, all the doers of bad deeds that harm the public are imprinted in the imagining and remembering brain, and they loathe them and seek tactics to be rid of them.

Hence, they praise and glorify the doers of the beneficial acts, to motivate them increasingly to these acts. This is where ideals, idealism, and every good attribute come from, as well as the wisdom of ethics.

Conversely, they will vehemently condemn the doers of detrimental actions, so as to stop and be rid of them. This is provenance of every evil trait, sin, and ignobility in the human species. Thus, individual opinion operates just like public opinion. Yet, this is true only with regard to benefit and harm.

THE CORRUPTION IN PUBLIC OPINION

The corruption in public opinion is that the public is not arranged according to its majority, but only according to the powerful, meaning the assertive. It is as they say, that twenty people rule all of France. In most cases, they are the rich, which are but ten percent of the public, and they are always the ignorant among the people (even in the eyes of the public).

They harm the public and exploit them. Hence, the public opinion is not in control of the world whatsoever. Rather, it is the opinion of the detrimental that controls the public. Thus, even the idealists that were sanctified in the world are but demons and evildoers regarding the majority of the public. Not only religion, but justice, too, is favoring the rich alone, all the more so ethics and ideals.

THE ORIGIN OF DEMOCRACY
AND SOCIALISM

This is where the idea of democracy stems from, so the majority of the public will take the judicial system and politics into their own hands. Socialism also, calls for the proletariat to take their destiny into their own hands. In short, the majority wants to determine public opinion, decide between beneficial and detrimental for them, and determine all the laws and ideals accordingly.

THE CONTRADICTION BETWEEN DEMOCRACY AND SOCIALISM

The contradiction between democracy and socialism, as seen in Russia, is that ten percent control the entire public in absolute dictatorship. The reason is simple: Just division requires idealism. This is not found among the majority of the public. Hence, ultimately, there is no cure for this except through religion, from above. This will turn the entire public into idealists.

[new page]

CONTACT WITH HIM

People imagine that a person who has contact with the Creator is a person ... nature, and that they should fear speaking to Him, much less be in His immediate vicinity. It is human nature to fear anything outside the nature of creation. People are also afraid of anything uncommon, such as thunder and loud noises.

However, He is not so. This is because in fact, there is nothing more natural than coming into contact with one's maker, for He has made nature. In fact, every creature has contact with his maker, as it is written, "The whole earth is full of His glory," except we do not know or feel it.

Actually, one who is awarded contact with Him attains only the awareness. It is as though one has a treasure in his pocket, and he does not know it. Along comes another and lets him know what is in his pocket. Now he really has become rich.

Yet, there is nothing new here, no cause for excitement. In fact, nothing has been added in the actual reality. The same is true with one who has been granted the gift of knowing that he is the Creator's son: nothing has changed in his actual reality, but the awareness he had not had before.

Consequently, the attaining person even becomes more natural, simpler, and most humble. It might even be said that before the endowment, that person and all the people were outside of the simple nature. This is because now he is equal, simple, and understands all people, and is very much involved with them. There is no one closer to the folk than he, and it is only him that they should love, for they have no closer brother than him.

[new page]

REBUILDING THE WORLD

See "Personal Opinion and Public Opinion," and "The Contradiction between Democracy and Socialism."

It has been clarified there that until now public opinion evolved and was built according to the powerful ones in society, meaning the assertive. It is only recently that the masses have evolved through religion, through schools, and revolutions, and have perceived the method of democracy and socialism.

However, according to the natural law that "a wild ass' colt is born a man," and man is an upshot of a wild animal, and a monkey, it is according to Darwin's method or that of our sages. After the sin, the human species decline into monkeys, for "All before Eve are as a monkey before the man." However, according to man's merit, who consists in intellectual preparation, he continued to develop through deeds and suffering, and assumed religion, politics and justice, and finally became civilized. Indeed, this entire development was placed solely on the shoulders of the better part of society, and the masses followed them like a herd.

When the masses opened their eyes to take their fate into their hands, they had to revoke all the corrections and laws of the assertive, being religion, justice, and politics. This is because these were only according to the spirit of the assertive, according to their development and for their own good.

Thus, they had to build the world anew. In other words, they are like prehistoric people, the Darwinian ape, because they are not the ones who experienced these experiences, which brought them their measure of development. Until today, the succession of development was solely on the shoulders of the assertive, not on the masses, who, until now, were virgin soil.

Thus, the world is now in a state of total ruin. It is very primitive in the political sense, as in the age of the cavemen. They have not been through the experiences and actions that brought the assertive to take upon themselves religion, manners, and justice.

Hence, if we let the world develop naturally, today's world must undergo all the ruin and torments that the primitive man experienced, until they are compelled to assume permanent and beneficial political justice.

The first fruit of the ruin came upon us in the form of Nazism, which is ultimately merely a direct offshoot of democracy and socialism, meaning of the leadership of the majority, once the restraints of religion, manners, and justice have been removed.

NAZISM IS NOT AN OFFSHOOT OF GERMANY

It turns out that the world erroneously considers Nazism a particular offshoot of Germany. In truth, it is the offshoot of a democracy and socialism that were left without religion, manners, and justice. Thus, all the nations are equal in that; there is no hope at all that Nazism will perish with the victory of the allies, for tomorrow the Anglo-Saxons will adopt Nazism, since they, too, live in a world of democracy and Nazism.

Remember that democrats, too, must renounce religion, manners, and justice like the Marxists, because all these are loyal servants of only the assertive in the public. They always place obstacles before the democrats, or the better part [majority] of the public.

It is true that thinkers among the democrats keep a watchful eye that religion and manners are not destroyed at once, for they know that the world will be ruined. However, to that extent they also interfere with the government of the majority. Once the majority grows smart and understands them, it will certainly elect other leaders, such as Hitler, since he is a genuine representative of the majority of the public, be it German, Anglo-Saxon, or Polish.

THE ONE COUNSEL

Unlike the democrats—who wish to cancel religion and manners gradually, and adapt a new politics in a manner that will not ruin the world—the masses will not wait for them at all. Rather, as our sages say, "Do not ruin a synagogue before you can build a new one in its place."

In other words, we are forbidden to let the powerful ones [majority] take hold of the leadership before we build a religion, conducts, and politics suitable for them, because in the meantime the world will be ruined and there will be no one with whom to speak.

NIHILISM

[a philosophical view that negates all the traditional values and institutions]

Not complete nihilism, but nihilism of values (such as Nietzsche with regards to the values of Christianity), meaning all the values in the religious conducts, ethics, and politics that have been thus far accepted in the perception of humanism.

All these are compromises in the measurements of egoism of the individual, the state, or God's servant. And I say that any measure of egoism is faulty and detrimental, and there is no other arrangement except altruism, in the individual, the public, and the Lord.

MATERIALISTIC MONISM

Substance fathers everything, and thought is the result of actions and sensations, much like a mirror. There is no freedom of will, only freedom of deeds. However, not by itself, for evil deeds induce evil deeds, and the freedom of deeds is perceived by looking (in the mirror of called upon actions) through another person's mind. Then one has the freedom to obey it. And he will not be able to choose from his own (mirror) mind, since every man's way seems right in his own eyes, and his mind always consents.

OUTSIDE OF THIS WORLD

Outside of this world we must research and examine only subjectively and pragmatically (practically). This way is the conduct of the research in this world, though it is outside of it, as it contemplates by measurements clothed in the nature of this world, and also according the practical (pragmatic) benefit.

WHAT IS OUTSIDE OF THIS WORLD?

Only the Creator is imperative, since He is the place of the world, and the world is His place. It is He alone that we understand, that He is also outside of this world, and nothing else, unlike pantheism.

This world is an objective term, which can be comprehended objectively as well. Its first principles are "time" and "space." Outside of this world, which are the worlds of *AK* and *ABYA* [the worlds *Adam Kadmon, Atzilut, Beria, Yetzira,* and *Assiya*], only subjective comprehension is possible, without touching the object whatsoever.

The essence of the objects we define by the names *ABYA* follow the assumption that since everyone perceives so without exception (meaning a chosen few in each generation, which are the tens of thousands and the millions that were, and are destined to come). Thus, we have objective attainment there, though we do not touch the objects whatsoever.

From here come the four worlds above this world, though by nature they are only subjective, clothing the natures of this world in the two ways—expansion and thought, namely psychophysical parallelism. This is so because we know any object by two forms: physical first, and psychic next, and they always go together, in a parallel manner.

It is known that many in this world, too, perceive the method of "expressionism," meaning solely by subjective perception. However, I also conform to "impressionism" to explain concepts of this world as objectively as possible, minimizing the interference of subjective reinforcement.

[new page]

THE ESSENCE OF RELIGION

The essence of religion is only understood pragmatically, as written by James [William James (1842-1910), American philosopher]. The origin of faith is in the need for the truth in it, inasmuch as it satisfies this need.

There are two kinds of needs: 1) A mental need. Without it, life would become sickeningly detestable. 2) A physical need. This need appears primarily in the social order, such as in ethics and politics, as Kant [German philosopher (1724-1804)] had written, "Faith is the basis of morality, and guards it."

Naturally, sages will come solely from among those with the mental need, for they also need it objectively. However, the second part will derive satisfaction, namely truth, also subjectively. However, from *Lo Lishma* [not for her sake] one comes to *Lishma* [for her sake]. The need comes before the reason that necessitates faith.

THE LEADERS OF THE PUBLIC

For oneself, one may choose between expressionism and impressionism. However, the leaders are not permitted to lead the public in any other way but a positive and pragmatic one, meaning according to expressionism. This is because they cannot harm the public for their personal interest.

For example, they cannot instruct a certain faith to the public in order to understand their own impressionism, thus denying moral conduct and ethics from the public. If one cannot control oneself, he had better resign and not harm the public with his ideals.

PERCEPTION OF THE WORLD

The world was created through consequential evolution, according to historic materialism and the dialectics of Hegel [Georg Wilhelm Friedrich Hegel (1770-1831), German philosopher] of thesis, antithesis, and synthesis. Indeed, it corresponds to the sensation of the Creator, from the still, vegetative, animate, and speaking, up to prophecy, or to the knowledge of God. Pleasure is the thesis, affliction is the antithesis, and the sensation outside one's skin is the synthesis.

THE ESSENCE OF CORRUPTION AND CORRECTION IS IN THE PUBLIC OPINION

As private opinion determines one's own gains and losses and brings one to the most successful business, so public opinion determines the policy, and chooses the most successful. However, there is quantity and there is quality.

QUANTITY VS. QUALITY

Until now, the qualitative [powerful] (who are the assertive), determined and made the views of the entire public, and therefore all the justice and morality. Religion was used to harm the majority, which are 80% of society.

THE MAJORITY IS AS PRIMITIVE AS PREHISTORIC MAN

The majority is as primitive as prehistoric man. This is so because they have not tried to utilize justice, religion, and morality, which were used by others until today. However, of course, all these came to the present state only through great pains in the path of causality and dialectics. The majority paid no heed to it, and at any rate, cannot grasp it.

THE QUICKEST ACTION IS RELIGION

In order to activate public opinion anew in the majority in an effective manner, there is no quicker way than religion, the loathing of any measure of will to receive, and elevating the beauty of the will to bestow to a great extent. This must be done specifically by actions. Although the psychophysical are parallel, still, the physical precedes the psychic.

[new page]

THE PRODIGIES

The prodigies is a product of the generation, with a strong inclination to bestow, and does not need a thing for himself. As such, he has equivalence of form with the Creator, and naturally cleaves to Him. He extends wisdom and pleasure from Him and bestows upon humankind.

They are divided into two kinds: Either they work consciously, meaning to bestow contentment upon their maker, and hence bestow upon humankind, or they work unconsciously, meaning that they do not feel and know that they are in adhesion with the Creator. They cleave to Him unconsciously. They only bestow upon humanity, and according to this principle, there is no progress to humanity, except to instill the will to bestow in them, and multiply the prodigies in the world.

TELEOLOGY

[The science of purpose]

Teleology is necessary in Kabbalah, according to the method of anthropocentricity, that the worlds were created for Israel, and they are the purpose. Moreover, the Creator consulted with the souls of the righteous. Their purpose is also brought in the prophecy: "And the whole earth shall be full of the knowledge of the Lord." There is none more specific purpose than that.

Maimonides takes after the method of dysteleology, and says that the Creator has for creation other purposes besides the human species. It is hard for him to comprehend that the Creator has created such a great creation, with planetary systems, where our planet is like a grain of sand, and all this was only for the purpose of man's completeness.

Purpose is imperative for any mindful being, and one who works purposelessly is mindless. By His acts we know Him. He has created the world in still, vegetative, animate, and speaking. The speaking is the climax of creation, since it feels others and bestows upon them. Atop them is the prophet, who feels the Creator and knows Him. This is perceived as pleasing Him, and His purpose in the entire creation.

Hegel's question is that necessarily, there are purposeless creatures in nature, like many things on our planet, and the countless planets that humankind does not use at all. The answer is in accordance with the law that "The unknown does not contradict the known," and that "The judge has only what his eyes see." Perhaps there is still, vegetative, animate and speaking on each planet, and in all the planets, and its purpose is the speaking.

It is likewise with the unknown. And how can that contradict the known and familiar in the way of prophecy? This is simple: It is pleasurable for the Creator to create an object that will be qualified for negotiation with Him, and exchange opinions, etc. There is also pleasure in having something that is not of the same kind, and we completely trust the prophecy.

CAUSALITY AND CHOICE

There is a path of pain, by which one pays unconsciously by dialectic laws, where each being conceals the absence within. The being exists as long as the absence in it has not appeared. When the antithesis manifests and develops, it destroys the thesis, and brings in its place a more complete being than the first, as it contains the correction of the previous antithesis. (This is so because any absence precedes presence.) Hence, the second being is called "synthesis," meaning that it includes and is an upshot of both, the presence and the absence, which preceded this new being.

Likewise, truth always follows and is perfected by the path of suffering, which is presence and absence, thesis and antithesis, and always yields truer syntheses until the appearance of the perfect syntheses. But what is perfection?

In historic materialism, the above-mentioned path of suffering is clarified only with relation to economic desires, where each thesis means just governance for its time, each antithesis means unjust division in the economy, and each synthesis is governance that settles the antithesis that has been revealed, and nothing more. For this reason, absence is concealed in it, as well. When the absence develops, it destroys that synthesis, too, and so forth, until the just division manifests.

PATH OF TORAH

Path of Torah is placing fate in the hands of the oppressed. This accelerates the end to the extent that the oppressed watch over it. This is called "choice," since now the choice is in the hands of the concerned parties. Thus, the path of pain is an objective act, the path of Torah is a subjective act, and fate is in the hands of the concerned parties.

[new page]

The principle: bestowal upon others. The governance—a regime that mandates a minimum for life, and good deeds toward the standard of living of society. The purpose and the goal: adhesion with Him. In my opinion, this is the final synthesis where absence is no longer concealed.

GOOD DEEDS AND *MITZVOT*

Locke [John Locke (1632-1704), English philosopher] said that there is nothing in the mind that does not come in the senses first. In addition, Spinoza [Baruch Spinoza (1632-1677), Jewish Dutch philosopher] said, "I do not want something because it is good, but it is good because I want it." We must add to this there is nothing in the senses that is not present in actions first.

Thus, the acts beget senses, and senses beget understanding. For example, it is impossible for the senses to take pleasure in bestowal before they actually bestow. Moreover, it is impossible to understand and perceive the great importance of bestowal before it is tasted in the senses.

Likewise, it is impossible to taste pleasure in adhesion before one performs many good deeds that can affect it, meaning by strict observance of this condition to bring Him contentment, or in other words, delight in the contentment given to the Creator by performing the commandment. After one feels the great pleasure in the acts, it is possible to understand Him, to the extent of that pleasure. And if ... for eternal and perpetual pleasure from bringing contentment to Him, then he will be rewarded with knowing...

As seen above, there are two modes to religion: 1) *Lo Lishma* [not for her name], which is pure utilitarianism, meaning aiming to establish morality for one's own good. One is satisfied when acquiring this tendency. And there is a second tendency to religion, being a mental need to cleave to Him. This is called *Lishma* [for her name]. One can be rewarded with the above through actions, and from *Lo Lishma* one comes to *Lishma*.

LIFE'S TENDENCY

There are three views in books and in research: either ideas about how to attain adhesion with Him, or to acquire progress, called utilitarianism, or corporeal pleasure of the flesh, called Hedonism.

I wish the view of Hedonism were true. The trouble is that the pains are greater than the few sensual pleasures that one can delight in. Besides the flaw of the day of death, and the method of utilitarianism to bring progress to the world, there is a big question here: Who enjoys this complete progress that I pay so heavily for with pains and torments?

It seems that only ideals whose tendency is man's happiness, thereby improving all the mental forces, impart to one respect in life and a good name after his death. Kant mocked this method of establishing a moral thesis on an egoistic tendency and instructed doing in order to not receive reward.

Modern science has chosen for itself utilitarianism, but only for the common good, meaning to bestow. This is also similar to "in order to not receive reward," and who would want it? There is also the question: What will this progress bring to the generations for which I work with so much pain to give this?

At the very least, I have the right to know what is required of progress, and who one will enjoy it. Who would be so gullible as to pay so heavily without knowing its effect? The whole trouble is that the pleasure is brief and the suffering, long.

Life's Purpose

From all the aforementioned, you will find that life's direction is to attain adhesion with Him, strictly to benefit the Creator, or to merit the public to achieve adhesion with Him.

Two Enslavements in the World

There are two enslavements in the world, either enslavement to the Creator, or enslavement to His creatures. One of them is a must. Even a king and a president necessarily serve the people. Indeed, the taste of complete freedom is only to one who is enslaved to the Creator alone, and not to any being in the world. Enslavement is necessary, for reception is obscene; it is beastliness. And bestowal, the question is "To whom?"

Part Three

Section One

Pragmatic Communism

Accepting the religion of "Love your neighbor as yourself," literally.

Just division of the profits, where each will work according to his ability, and receive according to his needs.

Property is kept, but its owner is forbidden to receive from the profits more than he actually needs. One type of property owners will be kept under public supervisors, another type by self-fiduciary, or books.

The unemployed will receive their needs equally with the employed.

Those who live in communes will earn the same wages as workers who are property owners, and the profits made by the communal life will be made into public property belonging to the members of that collective.

There must also be an effort to build communal life for workers in towns.

Advantages

The workers, and even more so those who are afraid of being unemployed, will certainly assume the religion, thus acquiring security in their lives. The idealistic property owners will also assume the religion by indoctrination on a religious basis.

Public opinion must be such that one who takes more than one needs is like a murderer. Because of him, the world will have to continue with the slaughter, Hitlerian manners, and terrible wars. Thus, communism will be promoted.

It is possible to make the life of property owners miserable by contracts and strikes, so they assume the religion since they do not touch their properties, only the profits. Since the religion will be international, it will be possible to win the hearts of the Arab Sheiks with money and religious influence --- so they assume the religion together with us as one unit, and promote it among the Arab workers and property owners.

That, in turn, will benefit Zionism. Because they will assume the religion that necessitates love and bestowal upon all humankind equally, they will not be envious of the robbing of the land, since they will understand that the land is the Lord's. The standard of living of the Arabs will be equal to the standard of living of the Jews. This will be a great incentive in winning their hearts.

SECTION TWO

Private Opinion and Public Opinion

As there is private opinion, which is one's judgmental force where all the good and bad actions are copied, and as one chooses the good and rejects the bad as though looking in a mirror, so is there a collective intellect to the public, where the good actions for society and bad ones are copied. Public opinion sorts out the ones that are good for it, praises their doers, and condemns those who do otherwise. From here emerge ideals, leaders, rules, and preferences.

The Corruption in Public Opinion: the Powerful Ones

Until today, only the assertive had the judgment and the force to lead, being the better part, as it is said, that twenty people lead all of France, and they make public opinion. They have arranged justice, morality, and religion to their benefit. Since they exploit the majority of the public, the religion, law, and ethics are hence detrimental to the public, meaning to the majority.

Bear in mind that the current government of the assertive was quite sufficient until today because the masses did not have any force of judgment. Thus, all the ruins preceding today's political order were only among the assertive. However, they did not come to the present order within one generation's time, but through terrible ruins, until they have conceived the religion, ethics, and law that have brought order to the world.

The New Structure

In recent generations, due to pressure and necessity, and through democracy and socialism, the masses have begun to open their eyes and assume responsibility for the management of society by the majority. Thus, they have concluded that religion, manners, governance, and justice are all to their detriment, as it is true that it serves the assertive ten percent of the public, and harms all the others.

Thus, two images of collective government emerged: either as the Nazis, who have rebelled against religion, manners, and justice, and do as the primitive man, prior to the conducts of life of the assertive, or as the Soviets, where ten percent of the public controls the entire public by dictatorship. This will certainly not last long, in light of the historical dialectic.

If manners are revoked, Israel's enemies will wipe out everyone. In short, we will necessarily and undoubtedly return to being cave dwellers, until (the masses, too) the majority learn the dialectics on their own flesh and bones (as did the powerful ones before them), and finally agree to order.

Thus, Nazism Is Not a German Patent

If we bear in mind that the masses are not idealists, then there is no counsel but religion, from which manners and justice naturally emanate. However, now they only serve the majority. How so? Through the religion of bestowal.

The principle of bestowal upon one's fellow person. The leadership: commitment to a certain minimum, and commandment for a standard of living.

The goal: adhesion with the Creator.

Nazism Is the Fruit of Socialism

Idealists are few, and the true carriers, the workers and the farmers, are egoists. If a preacher such as Hitler were to arise in any nation, saying that National Socialism is more convenient and beneficial to them than internationalism, why would they not listen to him?

[new page]

1) If Nazism and its ruin had been conceived some years back, and if some wise men were to devise a plan to save them through devout religion that would suffice for protection, would it have been forbidden in the name of falsehood?

2) If, after the war, the nations come to an understanding that Israel must be dispersed to the four corners, and drive us out of our land, and a certain person would come and reinstate religion (so as to stand devotedly) between us and the nations, thus making them agree to the opposite, that even the Diaspora would come to Israel, would that have been forbidden?

3) If the Nazis, God forbid, prevail and rule the world, and wish to destroy the residue of Jacob, is it permissible to institute religion among all nations in order to save the nation?

Pragmatism

Faith stems from a need; it is true as long as it satisfies that need (James [William James]). Thus, the need is the reason for faith, and the satisfaction of the need is its trueness.

Two needs: 1) A material need to establish social life; this is its trueness. 2) A mental need, without which life is loathsome; this is *Lishma* (for her name).

Of course, the sages of religion come from the mental need, but from *Lo Lishma* [not for her name] one comes to *Lishma* (see "Pragmatic Truth").

Life's Direction:

1) To bring progress and happiness to society through modern science.

2) By perfecting all of one's mental powers, one will attain dignity in life and a good name after death. Kant mocks it as egoism, and indicated that only not in order to receive reward.

We must understand: If it is not worthwhile to live for myself, is it worthwhile to live for a thousand others like me, or a billion? Thus, the direction must be to benefit the Creator, whether for oneself, or for the entire world, to award them adhesion with Him.

Truth and Falsehood

Truth and falsehood are a psychic replica of existence and absence, which are thesis and antithesis, from which stem the "ephemeral truth," which is a synthesis. This is a pragmatic truth, lasting until the "absolute truth" appears, where there will be no falsehood in one's conscience.

Example no. 4 (see above): Would ancient, primitive humanity, which slaughtered and killed each other like wild animals, permit the institution of a religious government?

Example no. 5 (see above): In my childhood I did not want to read novels so as not to deal with lies. I read only history. When I grew up and understood the value of them, that they develop the imagination, they became truth for me.

[new page]

Necessity

From the perspective of *Lishma* [for her name], it is an emotional need. Admittedly, they are few, as it is written, "saw that the righteous are few... and planted them in every generation," that they may have demand from birth. However, some abhor material life. If they do not accomplish the goal of adhesion, they will commit suicide.

The Religious Principle: from Lo Lishma [not for her name], one comes to Lishma [for her name]

Providence has prepared the guidance of people in an egoistic manner, which would necessarily induce the destruction of the world, unless they accept the religion of bestowal. Hence, there is a pragmatic need for it, and from that, one comes to *Lishma*.

What Is an Emotional Need?

As a blind person cannot perceive color, or a eunuch the joy of sex, it is impossible to depict this need to one who lacks the emotional need. And yet, it is a must.

Performing *Mitzvot* [commandments]

Performing *Mitzvot* can become for one an emotional need.

Morality of Manners

Morality of manners means good attributes not in order to be rewarded, and without external necessity, but based solely on altruism and a sense of responsibility for human society. It is achieved by education. However, education requires public approval to keep and sustain it after one departs from under the authority of the education. But public opinion does not stem from the education, but only from the benefit of the public.

The benefit of the public is evaluated only according to the specific state of that public, which is necessarily in contrast with other states and countries. Hence, how will education help in that? The proof is that the manner, and even the religion, sufficient for internationality, has not been created, as killing and looting rule everywhere, without any manners whatsoever. Moreover, the greater murderer one is, the more patriotic and well mannered he is considered. And today, it is international manner that we need.

Public Egoism Can Be Corrected Only by Religion

Public egoism can be corrected only by religion because education that is based on nothing can be easily ruined by any wicked person, and Germany is the evidence. If Hitler occurred in a religious Germany, he would not have done a thing.

Natural Egoism

You will not break natural egoism with artificial means such as public opinion and education. There is no cure for that but a natural religion.

Double Benefit

The religion of bestowal is salutary for both the body and the mind; hence, it is necessitated and agreed upon more than any method in the world (see below at length).

Motive Power

There are two discernments in it: The attracting force, from before, or the repelling force, from behind.

How can education help when one is free, without any motivation for the duties he was brought up on? After all, there is no attracting force in them, and they are also devoid of the compelling force.

[new page]

The Remaining of the Soul

This is a given, as it is a part of God above. However, it is not included in the wisdom of Kabbalah because no object is attainable. Indeed, the soul appears to the person who carries it only through actions, and its actions are only attainments of Him.

It is therefore clear that the maxim, "Know yourself and know all," is from ... philosophical because in Kabbalah the opposite should be said, "Know everything and ... attain yourself." An object is not attained at all, only actions, which are attainments of His names, meaning only subjective.

Five Senses

The power in commandments is similar to corporeality, where the actions stimulate the senses. And when the senses remain ... in the memory brain, they become there images of beneficial, detrimental, and property. And when the mind or the will or the guard ... looks in the image of the memory, one gradually scrutinizes the images and brings the truths closer, meaning the beneficial or the property, and rejects the falsehoods, which are the detrimental.

Man's knowledge grows according to the clarity of the scrutiny. And if in mathematics, he should attach to it images that are beneficial for clarity and validity. They also save time because these help him, as in existing property. The same goes for playing music, healing, and an attribute.

It is similar with spiritual works, which ... the commandments that stimulate man's spiritual senses. There are two kinds of senses here: either sight, hearing, smell, and speech, which are ord ... and also *HGT NH* [*Hesed-Gevura-Tifferet Netzah-Hod*] of the body. It is so because perpetuation of good deeds from ... in one who works the spirit of "love," and when it accumulates into a sizable amount ... in him the sense of "fear" of sinning and losing the love. And when he is cer ... of himself that he has the sense of love and fear, a sense of boas ... over his friends who were not rewarded with it is born in him (and this is property).

And following the three senses ... the "eternity" is born in him as a mighty one who controls his spirit. And according to all the sensations of these four senses, "glory" is born in him as he admits the existence of the Creator.

And with each commandment that he adds, the five above-mentioned lower senses and the flavors of the commandments intensify in him. When they accumulate to the required amount, the five higher senses, sight-hearing-smell-speech, are born in him, to actually see His glory and hear the voice of the Creator, smell the fear of Him, and speak before Him.

And when one is rewarded further, images of the impressions of the five lower senses and the five upper sense remain in him, and he looks as though through the mirror of the brain at these impressions, and sorts out the beneficial and the ... and rejects the detrimental. And according to the clarity of the scrutinies, the knowledge of the Creator will increase.

Luxury and Accumulated Property

As in corporeality, so in learning. ...In external teachings there is economics. ...And medicine is regarded as scrutinies that help the standard of living for ... as luxury. This is the first degree of property. The second degree is accumulating property, which is not as usable as wealth. This is the science of ... and an attribute, and playing music.

Likewise, in spirituality, the scrutinies that can be used ... are for a spiritual standard of living, and a non-accumulating property.

There are also higher scrutinies that do not serve for the standard of living, but only as accumulating properties and for important possessions such as wealth and the attribute, and philosophy.

However, both come from spiritual images that were once absorbed in the senses. And choosing the beneficial for oneself or for others is called "the knowledge of the Creator." Know that the wisdom of Kabbalah also contains these three kinds of property.

Psychophysical Parallelism

These are two manifestations of the same entity, like thunder and lightning. This is the meaning of "good deeds and Torah." However, a person first feels the psychic explanation, and then the physical one. It is similar to love, where the giver of the present first feels with one's mind that the giver loves him, and then sparks of love flow and spread through him. ...A revealing head is psychic, and inside, it clothes...

[new page]

The Root Cause of Every Error in the World

The root cause of every error in the world is an idea—when taking an idea or an image that was once clothed in a body, and presenting it as an abstract object that has never been in a body. That is, it is when it is praised or condemned according to that abstract value.

The problem is that once the concept has been stripped of a body, it loses significant parts of its initial meaning while it was clothed in a body. Those who discuss it according to its remaining meaning must necessarily misunderstand.

For example, when truth and falsehood work in the body, we praise the truth according to its benefit to the individual or to the ... and we condemn the lie according to its harm to the collective or to the individual. However, once truth and falsehood have been stripped of the bodies and become abstract concepts, they lose the heart of their meaning ... and acquire sanctity or impurity in their abstract form.

And according to ... it is possible for the evaluator to praise the truth even when it does great harm to the collective or to the individual, and to condemn ... the lie even when it is extremely beneficial to the individual or to the collective. This is a grave mistake that harms the ... and one is not free to ask oneself who sanctified this truth, or ... defiled and forbade this lie.

Benefit, in Fact, Everyone Admits It

Those who dispute it, it is ... that they benefit ... and a moral conduct that at times contradicts the physical benefit. However, essentially, moral and religion are also utilitarian. ... everything, except spiritual happiness, and what is the difference?

There is not a fool who will exert without benefit for the body or the mind.

Double Benefit

Accordingly, the law of bestowing upon others is necessary for all the people in the world ... as it is beneficial for both the body and the soul according to the wisdom of Kabbalah.

[new page]

A Vague Complex that Must Be Resolved One at a Time

The main problem is that here there is a ... complicated made of several interweaving doubts:

First: Even when not taking into account the validity, the question remains whether it is actually beneficial.

Second: Even if it is beneficial, is it feasible?

Third: Who are the people to be qualified for training the generation to such a sublime matter?

Fourth: Perhaps this operation will evoke the public's contempt and mockery?

Knowing

Knowing comes in one of three ways: empirical, which is by physical observation (actual experiments), historic, using documents and papers, or mathematical, by joining of sizes and templates (through knowing)...

And the wisdom of Kabbalah is more confirmed than all three above-mentioned ways.

There is also a fourth way to know—through philosophical deductions, either by deductions or by inductions, meaning from the general to the particular, or from the particular to the general. This is strictly forbidden in the wisdom of Kabbalah, since all that we do not attain, we do not know...

Part Four

SECTION ONE

The scrutiny that now, too, we are giving and are not receiving both because we are not taking the surplus we produce to the grave, and 2) because if a day's exertion awards half a day's pleasure, it is bestowal. And since by and large there is very little pleasure from the exertions people make, we are all only bestowing and not receiving. This is a mathematical calculation.

3) The clarification that we exert today due to the enslavement of society at least 14 hours a day with pain and sorrow, since all our customs come from enslavement to the public.

... The clarification that if we use the "governance of the earth," we can hasten the "last generation" in our generation, too.

4) This matter of competition out of uniqueness, in bestowal upon others is not an abstract fantasy, as it is used in practical life, such as those who give away all their possessions to the public, or the most idealistic members of parties, who neglect and lose their lives for the public's benefit, etc.

[new page]

What is this like? It is like a wealthy man who had an old father whom he did not wish to support. He was tried and the verdict was that he would support him at least as respectfully as he supports his own kin, or he would face a harsh punishment.

Naturally, he took him into his home and had to support him generously, but his heart was grieving. The old man said to him, "Since you are already giving me every delight that you have on your table, what would you lose if you also had a good intention, which is reasonable in the eyes of every sensible person, to be happy with having the opportunity to honor your father, who had spent all his energy for you and made you a respectable man? Why are you so obstinate that you afflict yourself? Can you rid yourself even slightly because of it?"

So it is. At the end of the day, we bestow upon society, and only society gains from our lives, since every person, great or small, adds and enriches the treasury of society. But the individual, when weighing the sorrow and pain that one receives, one is in great deficit. Hence, you are giving to your fellow person, but painfully and with great and bitter suffering. So why do you mind the good intention?

SECTION TWO

[This section includes four segments
grouped together by context]

Each one of them fills his or her role in service of the public in the best way, albeit without seeing it, since public opinion presses a person even secretly, to the point where one feels that deceiving society by mistake is as grave as killing a human being by mistake.

Each country is divided into societies where a certain number of people with sufficient means to provide for all their needs connect into a single society.

Each society has a budget and work-hours according to the local conditions. Half of the budget is filled by mandatory hours, where each member commits to work a certain number of hours according to one's strength, and the other half by voluntary hours.

A person who has faltered with self-gain, that person's entire social status vanishes into the thin air of society as clouds in the wind, due to the profound antagonism that such a person receives from the entire nation.

*

For then each person

1) Each individual makes him or herself willingly available for the service of the public whenever one is needed.

2) Free competition for every individual, but in bestowal upon others.

3) Disclosing any form of desire to receive for oneself is dishonorable and such a great flaw that such a person is regarded as being among the lowest, most inferior people in society.

4) Each person is medium.

*

1) They have many methodical books of wisdom and morals that prove the glory and sublimity of excellence in bestowing upon others, to a point where the entire nation, from small to great, engage in them wholeheartedly.

2) Each person who is appointed to an important position must first graduate a special training in the above-mentioned teaching.

3) Their courts are busy primarily with awarding accolades marking the level of each person's distinction in bestowal upon others. There is not a person without a medal on the sleeve, and it is a great offense to call a person not by one's title of honor. It is also a great offense for a person to forgive such an insult to one's title.

4) There is such fierce competition in the field of bestowal upon others that most people risk their lives, since public opinion tremendously appreciates and respects the accolades of the highest rank in bestowal upon others.

5) If a person is recognized as having done for oneself a little more than what was decided for him by society, society condemns it so much that it becomes a disgrace to speak with him, and he also gravely blemishes his family name. The only remedy for this is to ask for the court's help, which has certain ways by which to help such miserable people who have lost their position in society. But for the most part, they relocate him because of prejudice, since public opinion cannot be changed.

6) There is no such word as "punishment" in the laws of the court, for according to their rules, the guilty ones are always the ones who gain the most. Thus, if one is guilty of

not giving all his work hours, then his time is either reduced or made easier, or the way he provides it is made easier for him. Sometimes he is given time to spend at school, to teach him the great merit of "bestowal upon others." It all depends on the view of the judges.

*

1) The state is divided into societies. A certain number of people, who can fully provide for themselves, may separate themselves and maintain a special society.

2) That society has a quota of work hours according to the conditions in which they live, meaning according to the local conditions and the preferences of the members.

This quota is filled by mandatory hours and voluntary hours. For the most part, voluntary hours are approximately half of the mandatory hours.

The work hours come from four types and are divided into works according to strength: The first type is the weak; the second type is the medium; the third type is the strong; and the fourth type is the quick.

For the work of one hour of type one, type two works two hours, type three four hours, and type four six hours.

Each person is trusted with finding one's appropriate type of work that suits one's strength.

Section Three

1) Introduction: Humanity's progress is a direct result of religion.

2) The process of religion in circles comes when at a low point comes the destruction of humanism to the extent

of the ruin of religiousness. For this reason, they accept religion against their will, the upward movement begins anew, and a new circle is formed.

3) The size of the circle corresponds to the genuineness of the religion that is regarded as the "basis" at the time of the ascent.

Plan A

Just as we expect actors in the theatre to do their best to make our imagination think that their acting is real, we expect our interpreters of religion to be able to touch our hearts so deeply that we will perceive the faith of religion as the actual reality. The shackles of religion are not at all heavy for those who do not believe, since the demand in commandments between man and man is accepted anyhow, and between man and God, a few commandments observed in public—such as those at one's disposal—are enough.

Plan B

Nature in *Gematria* is *Elokim* [God]. Therefore, everything that nature mandates ... the word of the Creator. The benefit of society is the reward and the damage to society is the punishment.

Accordingly, there is no point turning God into nature, meaning [a cut up word in the manuscript] a blind Creator who does not see or understand the work of His hands. We are better off, and it makes sense to every healthy person, that He sees and knows everything, for He punishes and rewards, since everyone sees that nature punishes and rewards. And Hitler will prove.

Plan C

All of the anticipated reward from the Creator, and the purpose of the entire creation, are *Dvekut* [adhesion] with the Creator, as in, "A tower filled abundantly, but no guests." This is what they who cling to Him with love receive.

Naturally, first, one emerges from imprisonment, which is emerging from the skin of one's body by bestowal upon others. Subsequently, one comes to the king's palace, which is *Dvekut* with Him through the intention to bestow contentment upon one's maker.

Therefore, the bulk of commandments are between man and man. One who gives preference to the commandments between man and God is as one who climbs to the second degree before he has climbed to the first. Clearly, he will break his legs.

Faith in the Masses

It is written, "The voice of the people is the voice of the Almighty." Indeed, this means that according to reality, they have chosen the least of all evils, and to that extent they always follow the good path. However, of course we must change reality so they can accept the utterly complete path. And it is true that the power of keeping in the masses in general chooses for them a way according to the situation. For this reason, once they have corrupted the interpretation of Torah and *Mitzvot* [commandments], they have become rebellious. However, it is a sacred duty to find a true interpretation in society, and then it will be to the contrary: The power of keeping in the masses will coerce the keeping of Torah and *Mitzvot*.

*

... public of the first degree.

To prepare the way he tried (its reason).

1. Nazism: egoism; the international: altruism.

2. It is possible to destabilize the Nazis only through a religion of altruism.

3. Only the workers are ready for this religion, as it is a revolution in religious perception.

4. This religious perception has three roles:

   i. a) To undermine the Nazis.

   ii. b) To qualify the masses to assume collective governance so they do not fail as the Russians have. (This follows the term: The progress of humanity comes only through religion.) It is so because the more the worker needs reward for the work, the regime cannot survive, as Marx said.

   iii. c) To take religion from the possessors and turn it into an instrument in the hands of the workers.

5. First, it will be accepted by the workers, and through them by the whole of Israel, and the same goes for the international of all the nations, and through them to all the classes among the nations.

6. Revolution in religious perception means that instead of the monks being thus far the destructors of the world, when they assume altruism, the monks will be the builders of the world, since the measure of anxiety can be measured only by the measure of help to society, in order to bring contentment to the maker.

7. This concept is clarified over nearly 2,000 pages that explain all the secrets of Torah that the human eye cannot see. It will make every person believe in its truthfulness, as they will see that they are the words of the Lord, for secrets of a glorious wisdom attributed to prophecy testifies to their truthfulness.

8. The distributor of religion must be capable of Plan A, to bring as much faith as possible to the people.

    In addition, he must bring complete sufficiency to the still, vegetative, animate, and speaking. Without it, religion is unsustainable. It is as Maimonides said, that it is like a line of blind people headed by one person who sees. That is, the speaking must stand at the front of the line at every place and in every generation. Hence, any religion that does not guarantee to elicit one man out of a thousand becoming a speaking, that religion is unsustainable.

9. Spreading the religion of love is done by Torah and prayer that can intensify one's quality of bestowal upon others. At that time, the Torah and prayer are as one who sharpens one's knife, so it can cut and finish one's work quickly. Conversely, one who works with a blunt knife believes it is better not to waste time sharpening the knife, and he is misled because his work becomes much longer.

(It is also clear with the regard to the term that there is no progress for humanity unless through religion.)

10. (Relates to item 9) The fourth role is in favor of Zionism, for during the truce, when fates of

123

countries are decided, we will not have those enemies from among the conservatives, who think we have no religion, as we learn from Weizmann's words [Chaim Weizmann (1874-1952), the first President of Israel], and the mediators are bound to be from among those conservatives.

Part Five

Do Not Destroy

The frivolous have already grasped that it is possible to be built, but only on the ruin of one's friend. This method is what fries humanity on fire to this day, since before one finds a vulnerable place in one's friend, one cannot even conceive building anything. But the minute one has found a weakness in one's friend's way, he will clasp there with his claws and venom until he destroys him entirely, and there he builds his palace of wisdom.

Thus, all the palaces of science are built in a place of ruin. And for this reason, every researcher is interested only in destroying, and the more one destroys, the more one is famous and praised. Indeed, this is the way that science develops, and it cannot be denied.

However, what is this like? It is similar to the struggle that ruled with its terrible destructions for eons before the land had formed over the sea. This, too, was certainly a kind of development. And yet, there is no reason to envy those people who witnessed those upheavals. Rather, we should be more envious of those who came to the world after the making of the peace, after the materials that struggled made peace, and each found its resting place on Earth as it is today.

And although the struggle persists today, it is nonetheless a minor struggle, and not upheavals where each one destroys its predecessor, who has become entirely exhausted. Rather, they have already understood that it is forbidden to destroy, since "for drowning others, you are drowned, and the end of those who drown you will be that they, too, will drown" (*Masechet Avot*, 2, 6). Rather, the struggle is more about weakening and restricting, while keeping the life of the weak and avoiding destroying it, for he knows full well that the tide will later turn, "And they who drown you will drown." It is similar to a war that the fighters will keep fighting, which is also for the same reason.

Now, if we really do learn from practical history, we must not overlook the above-mentioned principle, and we must take reality into consideration, as in a status quo, and punish one who murders a view just as we punish one who murders a person. It is so because a mind without a view is not in the type of emotion of pity, for they are more numerous than all the dunghills and the lakes, and all the air, and because of it they are given to Providence, and we have no tactics by which to assist them.

For this reason, we should presume that the land before us is vast, and there is room for all the views to dwell in it, the good as well as the bad. Indeed, one who kills and destroys a bad view is as one who destroys a corrected view, as there is no such thing as an "evil view" in the world. Rather, an unripe view is bad.

Therefore, we should judge it as one who kills a bad person, where "the voice of the blood of his descendants, and his descendants' descendants," we are redeemed from the evildoer. Likewise, a bad view is a seed that is still unripe for eating, but that will eventually grow and develop.

We should search for a new place for the palace of wisdom that we want to build, a place vacant of others' buildings, meaning without hurting any existing method. The mind is deep and broad, and the words of the wise are heard with pleasure, and the method of abusers and abused is agreed by everyone to be regarded as bad. Hence, this alone should be uprooted because it is obsolete and loathsome, according to everyone.

At the same time, we should keep all the manners of life in status quo and maintain the freedom of the individual, since they are not required for our new building because in the end it is merely an economic structure. It is similar to a merchant who wanted to open his own grocery store but feared the competition, so he burned all the stores in town along with the gold, jewels, gemstones, and clothes. He is too foolish because he will not grow any richer by burning the jewelry stores. Rather, grocery stores only would have been enough for his ruin, and let the keepers keep, and they who vacation, let them vacation. At most, one should establish a law that all who keep must add work so as to satiate the examiners.

[new page]

I know what Mark wrote, that once the wounds and troubles of the body have been bandaged we will begin, and we will have a suitable place for studying ideals. Besides, arguing that this is fundamentally untrue, since we know from experience that a tortured and afflicted body finds knowledge and truth better than a satiated body that knows no lack.

But even if we let his words be, we should still say, "Do not destroy." In the very least, it is similar to a person chopping off fruit trees because he wants to examine them so they will grow more fruitful. It is foolishness, for if he chops them off they will die and there will be no one picking fruits.

It is likewise in views that have come to us by inheritance from our fathers over hundreds of generations of development. He chops them off, dries them up, and ruins them, promising us that later, when he is at rest, he will examine them and will improve them, if possible. It is complete folly.

He assumes that religion harms the commune. (But how can he be certain of this assumption? After all, it is a view that is spreading among people of positivity and negativity, and many are the supporters.) He can only dispute the form of understanding that the abusers use to their own benefit. Therefore, we should fight for the understanding, so it does not harm, but sentence it a death sentence.

And yet, his whole theory is built only on religious hatred, similar to structures of contemporary scholars concerning hatred of religion, without any motive of economic damage. For this reason, we have permission to demand of the real sages, whose intention is only the economic side, to remove this item from their books. Only then will they have hope of winning a lasting victory that does not slide on its own vomit.

In a word, there is no joy without calamity, no good without bad. Even the wisest person cannot be saved from a medley of errors, and this is the weaker side in him, which leaves room for those who come to dispute him and finish him off. This is the weak side of Marxism, and it is why the occupation is difficult for them, and hundred fold so the right to exist.

Therefore, if you are true to your method and desire its persistence, hurry up and erase the above-mentioned item from your laws, and then your road will be safely paved.

Has Marx's Prophecy Come True?

On the one hand, his prophecy can be regarded as having been fully realized. The powerful people having been sitting for a while on the fear of certain ruin, on wondrous arms that have been accumulated, and of which there is not a shred of hope to be rid or to balance. Also, economists see their ruin in their eyes, and any chance for salvation has been quenched from reality. The hungry multitudes are accumulating in terrible masses each day; the working class has almost completed its ripeness, etc., etc.

Why Were They Cast to the Right?

On the other hand, we find the opposite. Fascism is growing daily, first Italy, now Germany, tomorrow Poland, and America is also on the verge, and so forth. It must be that that prophet had missed a point, which caused his grave error.

Buried in His Own Theory

But he is buried in his own theory, for he has added redundancies in the theory of participation, and these are the hard seeds that history cannot process whatsoever (religiousness and nationalism), and they were rejected to the right.

[new page]

Faulty Policy

The guard does not need to sit and guard the surpluses that do not concern his conservativeness, nor the freedom searcher need pursue freedom for the luxuries of the body, nor the collaborator needs to destroy the views that do not contradict his socialism.

All of these three methods are real and are equally respected by their proponents. If the forces let one sect destroy another for a time, it is an incarnation, and in the end, there must be laws that limit the types of arms, so one will not destroy the other to a greater extent. It is a circle, and one does not know what one's tomorrow will bring.

Therefore, before the day of struggle comes, there is time for the mind to protect from a complete ruin of one of the sides. The current power is not to be relied upon, but rather the certain future.

Considering the truth between the methods, I define this word according to the law of evolution, since each view and each method prepares and makes way for a better method. And as long as it is not made, it must be kept and persisted, since by destroying it you destroy the view and the method whose role is to yield its fruition.

Marx himself had pointed it out ... because he says that from the great bourgeoisie emerges the working class. Therefore, you will evidently see that if there had been a savior for the working class at the time, to destroy the great bourgeoisie, he would certainly obliterate the foundations of the commune from its root, for this strong law, "do not destroy," is telling you, until the time comes by itself. In that regard, I dispute him because he says that we must force the issue at all cost, and I say, except for the ruin of views, which do not need it whatsoever.

To everything, there is a time, and the time of socialism has arrived. Woe to the fools who miss out on the hour and place before them completely redundant obstacles and boundaries, which are as smoke in their eyes. For this reason, before they turn one way or the other, the world will have already overturned and they will find "relief and deliverance from another place," and they and their method will be lost for a long time.

The war over the definition of nationality is completely redundant and is nothing like private property. There is no private property in the spiritual, only in corporeal properties. One who does not desire the development of the wisdom, and who does not know that authors' envy increases wisdom? Therefore, no one disputes it even among the extreme leftist Marxists. Rather, the war concerns only the corporeal properties, for which envy yields nothing but fright and unnecessary agony. Hence, why should you fight spiritual properties and nationality?

Let us assume that all the nations have reached economic parity, and have annulled private property to such an extent that the existence of abusers is unthinkable. Instead of the nations competing with one another for corporeal assets, henceforth the competition will be over spiritual assets. That competition is bound to emerge in individuals, just as in the public. But here, no one speaks of it, even the most extreme, but would it be so.

Therefore, our debate revolves solely around spiritual assets from the past. You say that we permit the acquisition of such assets in the future with all the desirable and fitting freedom, but the past you take out of your houses. Is this not sick and twisted? After all, what will be permitted in the future, why should we destroy the great bulk that has been ready from the past? It is like that famous Egyptian king who inherited a library of precious books the size of three streets, and he commanded they be burned because they are not necessary for the existence of religion or for fear of harm.

And besides, no nation will obey your order to destroy all the assets of its past. They will fight over it with devotion (but you are absolutely permitted because you have no need for it at all). Indeed, even if a spirit of madness takes over the land to obey them to do this, they must spare this giant structure of several generations being lost for no reason at all.

Thus, you must leave the "You have chosen us" of each nation intact, to the extent that they want it. Only the corporeal basis of each nation should be abolished, since that basis has now reached its term, and it is in crisis by itself. For this reason, it might take correction from whichever hand reaches out to it. However, along with it we must give full and complete confidence to each and every nation that their spiritual assets will be kept in full.

We cannot argue about statements that oppose socialism as we do with religion, since both legislators and religious authorities admit that "renunciation of a court is renunciation, and the law of the land is the binding law." For this reason, all those laws that fundamentally oppose the socialism will remain as obsolete history, for now, too, there is already a large majority concealed and unused.

Before us are three forces in reality, fighting one another. And although it contradicts the view of Marxists, who take into account only two forces into consideration—abusers and abused—it is an abstract theory that has no more merit than all its preceding theories. However, according to the basis of Marxism itself, we should take into account only what is practical, not endless theories. This is why I have chosen to detect three forces as though they were set before our eyes in reality.

New Class Division: Quick and Idle

Let us assume that one nation is idle, and another nation is naturally more nimble. And what one does in two hours, the other does in an hour. Naturally, there will be complaints: One will say that all the nations should work the same number of hours, and the other will say that what counts is the amount they produce. And as it is with those who argue, each will insist. What is the foundation by which the court will decide? If it is according to the principle, "give as much as you can and receive as much as you need," it still does not necessitate an equal amount of time. And if we judge the nations according to the amount of work, then individuals, too, have a similar argument, and the diligent will work half as much as the weak. Thus, you have prepared for yourself a new class of quick, and a class of idle.

You could say that there is power in the idle majority to force the quick minority in the nation, but there is certainly no such power between the nations. Thus, you will create classes among the nations, and abusers and abused among individuals.

The Arrival of the Redeemer

This is not new, for the founders themselves knew it, as he says. ...that in the beginning they will see how this is possible through compromise, and will finally come to true ideals, to the highest degree of socialism, where each gives as much as he can, then takes only as much as he needs, meaning the same as the idle. This can be done only by the arrival of the redeemer, when the earth is full of knowledge. Then the giver will understand that he is exerting for his God, giving contentment to his maker.

[new page]

The idealistic instincts have already struck numerous roots in the human race. They have also come and become antiquated and have gained a foothold in a place where no one can reach, namely the subconscious in the elongated brain, which moves man's nerves by itself, without the person's awareness. This is why they have experimented in Russia, as it is known that they did not do a thing in all their wars. These warriors should know that the human heart will give them anything if they only leave it with its own ideals, which have come to it by inheritance from past generations in one's subconscious. If they insist on destroying this legacy, too, they themselves will suffer the consequences, for the heat and the sulfur is accumulating bit by bit until it is filled to the brim and begins to explode.

And besides all that, a new generation is growing, "which did not know Joseph." They do not understand at all the need and necessity to revoke private property from their flesh and blood, but only according to a dry theory. For this reason, the passion for private property that is buried deep in their subconscious from past generations, after all the learning, one fine day they will establish camps of young people from all sides, and they themselves will put the elderly to death with all their property and wisdom. It is so because an ideology does not come to a person from the intellect, but only from life's experiences, out of affection and a combination of good and bad, as with automatic machines. The mind has no control over the body, as it is completely foreign to us. Hence, those young socialists who have acquired knowledge through their own wit cannot be trusted whatsoever, and they will pop like a bubble of soap.

One Last Word of Policy

At that time, three forces will sit on the throne in the councils—right, left, and middle. They will argue and strife with one another: the right opposing the liberty in the left, and the left opposing the reactionism of the right, and the neutral will give room to both, and the majority will solve and determine.

Indeed, in one, they have already come to a solution, namely sharing all necessary and positive needs of life, meaning equal sharing of all the needs of the economy: one land to all who are living on it, and one division in its corporeal pleasures. All the trials and arguments they will load on the suffering of spiritual predicates, along with the three degrees—envy, lust, and honor—they will turn and restrict themselves only to the spiritual boundaries.

This version will indeed be the final word of policy because it will forever remain an inexorable law. It is so because according to the development of the human species, so will views separate and intensify, and each one will be far more obstinate than one is currently so about one's fortune. There is no hope to come out of this strait unless people begin to regress into the form of fools, meaning be emptied from all of their reason.

For this reason, there will be almost as many parties as there are people, and there is no solution to it other than the fixed law, "follow the majority." At that time people will make among them various compromises until they gather into groups. And in the groups, there will be competition with the oppositions until the opposition itself will separate.

Thus, the big groups will split into small ones, and the small ones into tiny ones, as well as trade among themselves, as is customary nowadays. However, this negotiation must acquire a more acrid form each time, precisely according to the measure of development of views without compromise forever, for so it should be forever.

[new page]

However, in one—in private property—they have already arrived at an agreed upon solution: Each will give as much as a successful one can give, and receive as much as an unsuccessful one, without adding even as much as a hairsbreadth. And the work hours will be equal to all, by order. And besides the obligation, there will be additional time to the veterans, who will give compared to the weak, to completely exempt them and not afflict them. This is similar to today's charity.

Also, in each city and community, the weak will be distributed equally. And if there are many volunteers in the community, then all the weak will be exempted. If there are few, then only some of them, the weakest, will be exempted.

One who breaks these rules will be punished either by giving his portion, or by criminal punishment.

The Anterior of an Idea

The truthfulness of the spirit of pleasure of one who expresses it is evident. I have become a c ... although ... [indecipherable words in the manuscript] many years prior, while I did not pay attention until I saw them speaking and arguing. Then I recognized the truth as it is. It is a law that one who is completely untroubled will not be satisfied by corporeal possessions. Even when engaged in an ideal, one must feel pleasure during the engagement. The measure of spirit and delight that one feels depends on the truthfulness of the ideal with which he is engaged.

Thus, we have found for truth an anterior face by which to know it, meaning by merely looking at the person who expresses it, whether he is enjoying or not. And the amount of pleasure is the amount of truth. This is what has brought me to believe in this idea, for until then I have never seen anyone to express any idea with such contentment and delight as they.

The Absolute Truth

If there are no absolute truths, but temporary ones, then I say that each truth in itself is the absolute truth for its time. It is just as it cannot be said about some reality that is about to die that it is regarded as dead, since while it is alive, it is an absolute reality.

[new page]

Everything is operated either voluntarily or by coercion, and the mind does not force. Therefore, we have a question: Who will move the socialist when he acts? What source will spur his desire to move, or by what force will coercion come upon him?

It is so because at that time, movement will become to him a kind of private property, and every person is meticulous about his energy, to not disperse it uselessly even more than for his fortune. And if the socialism is not because he is deficient, due to saving of energy, then he will certainly not squander the energy in vain. Thus, from where will justice or compassion come?

Rushing Its Ripening: through Religion

The socialistic ideal requires ripening in one's heart for at least three whole generations, and peace and general agreement. Therefore, many more attempts and cycles will the world endure before it comes to fruition, but there is no easier way to ripen the idea than through religion.

The Nation

המחיר 10 מיל

דו שבועון   בין מפלגתי

המערכת	מגמתנו
א. ג.	היחיד
שם האומה, השפה והארץ ____ יהא	
בקורת למרקסיזם לאור	
המציאות החדשה, ופתרון	
לשאלת אחוד האומה על	
זרמיה ____ יהא	
לשאלת היום ____ שלמה אשלג	
במה ציבורית ____ המערכת	

כתובת המערכת:
רחוב שלמה מס' 3 ת.ד. 5022
מחיר המודעות: האינטש 150 מיל
קבועות: לפי הסכם עם ההנהלה -

מחיר החתימה לשנה:
בארץ 400 בחוץ לארץ 2,50 דולאר
לחצי שנה 200 מיל

שנה א' גליון א'-ב   ירושלים   די סיוון, חש"ם.   5/6/1940

מגמתנו

עיתון זה "האמה" הוא יצור חדש ברחוב היהודי, עיתון שמטרתו הוא "בין מפלגתי". ואם משאלו, מה הפירוש של עיתון "בין מפלגתי"? איך יתואר עיתון, שיוכל לשמש כל המפלגות ביחד על אף כל הניגודים והסתירות שביניהם? אכן הוא מין בריאה, שנולדה בין המצרים בחבלי לידה קשים ואיומים, מתוך רעל השנאה שחף לאומות העולם להשמידנו מעל פני האדמה, כליון האיום של מיליונים מאחינו, ועוד ידם נטויה. יצר הסדיסטי שבהם לא ידע שבעה, ועוד האסון כפול, כי לא נוכל להשלות עצמנו, אשר כל זה הוא רק תופעה זמנית חולפת. כמו שמנוסים אנו ביותר בהיסטוריה, שאם אידה אומה התפרצה עלינו, מצאנו לה מחלץ באומה אחרת.

אבל עתה המצב משונה הוא לגמרי. כי מלבד שקיפנו אותנו בכח אחד מכל קצווי ארץ, הרי גם האומות העצלות ביותר, נעלו בעדינו את הדלתות, בלי רגש כל שגוא של חמלה ורחמים. ובאופן אכזרי כזה, שאין לו תקדים בכל המהליך של ההיסטוריה האנושית, אפילו בימים הברבריים ביותר.

והדבר ברור, אם לא לסמון על נסים, שקרומני, אם בחור יחיד אם בחור אומה, נמצא על כפות המאזנים של חיים ומות, וההצלה היא, אם נמצא

אם התחבולה הדרושה, דהיינו אומה חבולה הכבירה, שאין דרכה להימצא זולת בקרבם הסכנה, שמהיה בכוחה להכריע אם הכף לטובתנו, - לחם לנו כאן מקלט בטוח לכל פזורי אחינו, שלדברי הכול, הוא מקום ההצלה היחידה כעת. ואז דרך החיים תהיה פתוחה לנו, איך שהוא, להמשיך קיומנו על אף כל המעוקשים. ואם נחמיץ את השעה, ולא נקום כולנו כאיש אחד, במאמצים כבירים, הדרושים בעת סכנה, להבטיח לנו שארית בארץ, הרי העובדות שלפנינו מאיימות עלינו מאד, מאחר שהענינים מתפחחים כרצון אויבנו, האומרים להשמידנו מעל פני האדמה.

גם זה ברור, שלמאמץ הכביר הדרוש לנו בדרך התחחים שלעומתנו, צריכים אחדות אימנה ומוצקה כפלדה, מכל אברי האומה, בלי שום יוצא מהכלל. ואם לא נצא בשורות מלוכדות לקראת הכוחות האיתנים, העומדים לשם על דרכינו זה, נמצא מקורחינו גידדונו כאבודזו למפרע. ואחר כל אלה, כל אחד וכל מפלגה מאתנו, רובב ומשאר על רכבו הפלגתי בקפדנות יתחרה בלי וייתור כל שהוא, ובשום פנים לא יוכלו, או יותר נכון, לא ירצו לבוא לידי איחוד לאומי, כפי שדורש עם הסכנה שלעולינו. וכה אנו שוקעים באדישות, כאלו לא קרה מאומה.

המו"ל שלמה אשלג. העורך דר. י. בורג

דפוס הישראה ירושלים

Title page of *The Nation*

OUR INTENTION

This paper, *The Nation*, is a new entity on the Jewish street. It is an "inter-partisan" paper. And you may ask, "What does an 'inter-partisan' paper mean? How can there be a paper that can serve all parties together, despite all the opposition and contrasts among them?"

Indeed, it is a "being" that was born in dire straits, through hard and dreadful labor-pains, from amidst the venom of hatred that had struck the nations of the world to obliterate us from the face of the Earth, the destruction of millions of our brothers, and they are prepared to do more. Their sadistic inclination is insatiable, and the calamity is twofold, for we cannot delude ourselves that all this is but a passing, transitory phenomenon, as with our past experiences in history, that if a nation erupts on us, we find a substitute in another.

However, now things are very different. Not only are we simultaneously attacked from all directions, but even the most developed nations have locked their doors before us without any sentiment of mercy or compassion, and in such a ruthless manner that is unprecedented in the whole of human history, even in the most barbaric times.

It is clear, save for relying on miracles, that our existence as individuals or as a nation is hanging between life and death. And the salvation is if we find the required ploy, that great scheme whose way is only to be found near danger, and which can tilt the scale to our favor—to give us a safe haven here for all our brothers in the Diaspora, as everyone says it is, at present, the only place of salvation.

Then the road of life will be open to us, to somehow continue our existence despite the difficulties. And if we miss the opportunity and do not rise as one, with the great efforts required at a time of danger, to guarantee our staying in the land, then the facts before us pose a great threat to us, since matters are developing favorably for our enemies, who seek to destroy us from the face of the Earth.

It is also clear that the enormous effort that the rugged road ahead requires of us mandates unity that is as solid and as hard as steel, from all parts of the nation, without exception. If we do not come out with united ranks toward the mighty forces that are standing on our way to harm us, we will find that our hope is doomed in advance.

And after all that, each person and party sits and meticulously guards its own possessions without any concessions. And under no circumstances can they, or more correctly *want* to reach national unity, as this perilous time for all of us requires. Thus, we are immersed in indifference as though nothing had happened.

Try to imagine that if some nation "showed us the door," as is so common these days, it is certain that then none of us would think about our factional belonging, for the trouble would mold all of us into a single mush, to defend ourselves or to pack up and flee by sea or by land. Had we felt the danger as real, we would undoubtedly be properly united, too, without any difficulty.

Under these circumstances we have met here—a small group of us, from all sects, people who sense the dreadful whip on their backs as though it had already materialized. They had taken upon themselves to publish this paper, which they believe will be a faithful channel through which to convey their sensations to the whole nation, with all its sects and factions, none excluded. By doing so, the contrasts and the narrow-minded factionalism would be cancelled. More correctly, they would be silenced and make way to what precedes them, and we will all be able to unite into a single, solid body, qualified to protect itself at this crucial time.

And although this danger is known to all, as it is known to us, perhaps it has not yet sufficiently evolved in all the public, as it truly is. If they had felt it, they would have long ago shaken off the dust of factionalism to the extent that it obstructs the unity of our ranks. If this is not so, it is only because this sentiment is still not shared by many.

Hence, we have taken upon ourselves the publication of this paper, to stand guard, warn of the trouble, and explain it to the public, until all the segregating elements will be silenced, and we will be able to meet our enemy with united ranks, and give it its duly response in time.

Moreover, we are confident that among us there are still those who search the hearts, who can provide a successful scheme that will unite all the factions in the nation. From experience, we have learned that specifically those people go unnoticed and have no listeners. In this paper, we are willing to make room for anyone who carries a guaranteed solution for uniting the nation, to publicize it and to sound it in the public.

In addition to all the above, by publishing this paper, we aim to defend our ancient culture of two thousand years, since before the ruin of our country. We aim to reveal it, and clean it from the piles that have accumulated over it during the years of our exile among the nations, so that

145

their pure Jewish nature will be recognized, as they were at that time. This will bring us the greatest benefit, for we will be able to find a way to connect our Diaspora mode of thinking with that glorious time, and redeem ourselves from borrowing from others.

The Editors

THE INDIVIDUAL AND THE NATION

We humans are social beings. Because we cannot satisfy our vital needs without assistance from others, partnership with many is necessary for our existence. This is not the place to explore the evolutions of the nations, and we can suffice for studying reality as it appears to our eyes.

It is a fact that we cannot fulfill our needs by ourselves, and we need a social life. Hence, individuals were compelled to unite into a union called "a nation" or "a state," in which each engages in one's own trade, some in agriculture, and some in artisanship. They connect through trading of their products. Thus the nations were made, each with its unique nature, both in material life and in cultural life.

Observing life, we see that the process of a nation is just as the process of an individual. The functioning of each person within the nation is like the functioning of the organs in a single body. There must be complete harmony among the organs of each person—the eyes see and the brain is assisted by them to think and to consult, and then the hands work or fight, and the legs walk. Thus, each stands on its guard and awaits its role. Similarly, the organs that comprise the body of the nation—counselors, employers, workers, deliverers, etc.—should function in complete harmony among them. This is necessary for the nation's normal life and for a secured existence.

As the natural death of the individual results from disharmony among one's organs, the nation's natural decline results from some obstruction that occurred among its organs, as our sages testified (*Tosfot, Baba Metzia*, Chapter Two), "Jerusalem was ruined only because of unfounded hatred that existed in that generation." At that time, the nation was plagued and died, and its organs were scattered to every direction.

Therefore, it is a must for every nation to be strongly united within, so all the individuals within it are attached to one another by instinctive love. Moreover, each individual should feel that the happiness of the nation is one's own happiness, and the nation's decadence is one's own decadence. One should be willing to give one's all for the nation whenever needed. Otherwise, their right to exist as a nation in the world is doomed from the start.

This does not mean that all the people in the nation, without exception, must be so. It means that the people of that nation, who sense that harmony, are the ones who make the nation, and the measure of happiness of the nation and sustainability are measured by their quality. After a sufficient sum of individuals to the existence of the nation has been found, there can be a certain measure of loose limbs, which are not connected to the body of the nation in the above-mentioned measure, since the basis is already secured without them.

Hence, in ancient times, we did not find unions and societies without kinship among their members, since that primitive love, which is necessary for the existence of society, is found only in families that are offshoots of a single father.

However, as the generations evolved, there were already societies connected under the term "state," that is, without any familial or racial ties. The only connection of the individual to the state is no longer a natural, primitive connection, but stems from a common need where each individual bonds with the collective into a single body, which is the state. And the state protects the body and possessions of every individual with all the power of a state.

Indeed, that transition, where the generations moved from the natural nation to the artificial state, from ties that stem from primitive love to ties that stem from a common need, does not take anything from the conditions necessary in a natural, racial state. The rule is that as every healthy individual has complete control over one's organs, which is based solely on love, because the organs joyfully obey without any fear of punishment, the state should completely dominate all the individuals within it with respect to its general needs, based on love and instinctive devotion of the individuals to the collective. This is the most convenient force, sufficient to move the individuals toward the needs of the collective.

However, domination based on coercion and punishment is too weak a force to move every individual sufficiently to guard the needs of the public. The public, too, will weaken and will not be able to fulfill its commitment to guard and to secure each individual's body and possessions.

And we are not concerned with the form of governance of the state, whether autocratic, democratic, or cooperative. They do not change at all the essence of the establishment of the force of social unity. It cannot be established, much less persist, if not through ties of social love.

It is a shame to admit that one of the most precious merits we have lost during the exile, and the most important of them, is the loss of the awareness of the nationality, meaning that natural feeling that connects and sustains each and every nation. The threads of love that connect the nation, which are so natural and primitive in all the nations, have become degenerated and detached from our hearts, and they are gone.

And worst of all, even the little we have left of the national love is not instilled in us positively, as it is in all the nations. Rather, it exists within us on a negative basis: It is the common suffering that each of us suffers being a member of the nation. This has imprinted within us a national awareness and proximity, as with fellow-sufferers.

This is an external cause. As long as this external cause joined and blended with our natural national awareness, an odd kind of national love emerged and sparked off this jumble, unnatural and incomprehensible.

And most important, it is completely unfit for its task. Its measure of warmth suffices only to an ephemeral excitement, but without the power and strength with which we can be rebuilt as a nation that carries itself. This is because a union that exists due to an outside cause is not at all a national union.

In that sense, we are like a pile of nuts, united into a single body from the outside by a sack that envelops and unites them. Their measure of unity does not make them a united body, and each movement applied to the sack produces in them tumult and separation. Thus, they consistently arrive at new unions and partial aggregations. The fault is that they lack the inner unity, and their whole force of unity comes through outside incidents. To us, this is very painful to the heart.

Indeed, the spark of nationalism was kept within us to its fullest measure, but it has dimmed and has become inactive. It has also been greatly harmed by the mixture it had received from the outside, as we have said. However, this does not yet enrich us, and reality is very bitter.

The only hope is to thoroughly establish for ourselves a new national education, to reveal and ignite once more the natural national love that has been dimmed within us, to revive once more the national muscles, which have been inactive in us for two millennia, in every means suitable to this end. Then we will know that we have a natural, reliable foundation to be rebuilt and to continue our existence as a nation, qualified to carry itself as all the nations of the world.

This is a precondition for any work and act. In the beginning, the foundation must be built in a manner sufficiently healthy to carry the load it is meant to carry. Then the construction of the building begins. But it is a shame on those who build buildings without a solid enough basis. Not only are they not building anything, they are putting themselves and others next to them at risk, for the building will fall with the slightest movement and its parts will scatter to all directions.

Here I must stress concerning the above-mentioned national education: Although I aim to plant great love among the individuals in the nation in particular and for the entire nation in general, in the fullest possible measure, this is not at all similar to chauvinism or fascism. We loathe them, and my conscience is completely clear from them. Despite the apparent similarity of the words in their superficial sounds, since chauvinism is nothing but excessive national love, they are essentially far from one another as black from white.

To easily perceive the difference between them, we should compare them to the measures of egoism and altruism in the individual. As said above, the process of the nation is very similar to the process of the individual in all one's particular details. This is a general key by which to perceive all the national laws without deflecting right or left about them, even as a hair's breadth.

Clearly, the measure of egoism inherent in every creature is a necessary condition in the actual existence of the creature. Without it, it would not be a separated and distinct being in itself. Yet, this should not at all deny the measure of altruism in a person. The only thing required is to set distinct boundaries between them: The law of egoism must be kept in all its might, to the extent that it concerns the minimum existence. And with any surplus of that measure, permission is granted to waive it for the well-being of one's fellow person.

Naturally, anyone who acts in this manner is to be considered exceptionally altruistic. However, one who relinquishes one's minimal share, too, for the benefit of others, and thus risks one's life, this is completely unnatural and cannot be kept, but only once in life.

The excessive egoist, who has no regard at all for the well-being of others, is loathsome in our eyes, as this is the substance from which the looters, murderers, and all who are corrupt. It is similar with national egoism and altruism: The national love, too, must be imprinted in all the individuals in the nation, no less than the egoistic individual love in a person for one's own needs, sufficient to sustain the existence of the nation as such, so it can carry itself. And the surplus to that minimal measure can be dedicated to the well-being of humanism, to the whole of humanity, without any distinctions of nation or race.

Conversely, we are utterly hateful of the excessive national egoism, starting from nations that have no regard for the well-being of others, through ones that rob and murder other nations for their own pleasure, which is called "chauvinism." Thus, those who completely retire from nationalism and become cosmopolitan for humane, altruistic motives are making a fundamental error, since nationalism and humanism are not at all contradictory.

It is therefore evident that the national love is the basis of every nation, just as egoism is the basis of all individually existing beings. Without it, it would not be able to exist in the world. Similarly, the national love in the individuals of a nation is the basis of the independence of every nation. This is the only reason for which it continues or ceases to exist.

For this reason, this should be the first concern in the revival of the nation. This love is not presently within us, for we have lost it during our wandering among the nations for the past two millennia. Only individuals have gathered here, without any ties of pure national love among them. Rather, one is connected through a common language, another through a common homeland, a third through a common religion, and a fourth through common history. They all want to live here according to the measure by which they lived in the nation from which they came. They do not take into account that there it was a nation based on its own members before he or she had joined it, and which he or she took no active part in establishing it.

However, when a person comes to Israel, where there are no prearranged orders that suffice for a nation to function on its own, we have no other national substance on which structure we can rely, and we also have no wish for it. Rather, here we must rely entirely on our own structure; and how can we do this when there is no natural national connection that will unite us for this task?

These loose ties—language, religion, and history—are important values, and no one denies their national merit. However, they are still completely insufficient to rely on as a basis for the independent sustenance of a nation. In the end, all we have here is a gathering of strangers, descendents of cultures of seventy nations, each building a stage for oneself, one's spirit, and one's leanings. There is no elemental thing here that unites us all from within into a single mass.

I know that there is one thing that is common to all of us: the escape from the bitter exile. However, this is only a superficial union, like the sack that holds the nuts together, as was said above. This is why I said that we must establish for ourselves special education through widespread circulation, to instill in each of us a sense of national love, both from one person to another, and from the individuals to the whole, to rediscover the national love that was instilled within us since the time we were on our land as a nation among the nations.

This work precedes all others because besides being the basis, it gives the stature and successes to all the other actions that we wish to take in this field.

A.G.

THE NAME OF THE NATION, THE LANGUAGE, AND THE LAND

We should examine the name of our nation. We have grown accustomed to calling ourselves "Hebrews," while our usual names, "Jew" or "Israel," have all but become obsolete. It is so much so that to distinguish the jargon from the language of the nation we call the language of the nation "Hebrew," and the jargon, "Yiddish."

In the Bible we find the name, Hebrew, pronounced only by the nations of the world, and especially by the Egyptians, such as, "See, he has brought in a Hebrew unto us to mock us" (Genesis, 39:14), or "And there was with us there a young man, a Hebrew" (Genesis, 41:13), or "This is one of the Hebrews' children" (Exodus, 2:6). The Philistines also use this name: "Lest the Hebrews make a sword" (1 Samuel, 13:19). We also find it in the relation between the nations and us, such as in the war of Saul with the Philistines, when he declared, "Let the Hebrews hear," and "the Hebrews crossed the Jordan" (1 Samuel, 13:7).

Besides, we persistently find the name, "Hebrew," in proximity to slaves, such as a Hebrew slave or a Hebrew maidservant, etc. However, in truth, we will never meet in the Bible the name, "Hebrew," but only one of the two names, "Israel" or "Jew."

The origin of the name, "Hebrew," is that there was probably a famous ancient nation that went by that name, since the verse (Genesis, 10:21) presents before us the name of Noah's son as the father of that nation: "And unto Shem, the father of all the children of Ever." Abraham the patriarch was from that nation, which is why the nations called him "Abraham the Hebrew," such as "and told Abram the Hebrew" (Genesis, 14:13).

For this reason, before Israel became a nation among the nations, they were called "Hebrews," after the nation of Abraham the patriarch, the Hebrew. Although the children of Israel were distinguished in Egypt as a separate nation, such as "Behold, the people of the children of Israel are too many and too mighty for us; come, let us deal wisely with them, lest they multiply" (Exodus, 1:10). However, that name is as a name of a tribe, and not of a nation, for they became a nation only after they had arrived at the land of Israel. From this we should conclude that this is why the nations did not wish to call us "the Israeli nation" even after we had arrived at the land, so as not to admit our existence as a nation. They emphasized it by calling us "Hebrews," as they had called us prior to arriving at the land.

It is not by chance that the name, "Hebrews," is absent in the Bible and in subsequent literature, except in relation to servants and maidservants, to whom the name, "Hebrew," persistently clings: "Hebrew slave," "Hebrew maidservant." But we will never encounter an "Israeli slave" or a "Jewish slave." This juxtaposition is probably a relic of the slavery in Egypt, which we are commanded to remember (Deuteronomy, 5:15), "And you shall remember that you were a slave in the land of Egypt."

Even today the majority of nations refer to us as "Jews" or "Israelis," and only the Russian nation still relates to us as "Hebrews." Supposedly, the haters of Israel among them have installed this label among them with the ill-will of denying its nationalism from it, just as the ancient peoples. It seems that they had delved into the meaning of this name far more than we, who have taken it absentmindedly due to being used in the Russian language, without much examination. It follows from all the above that if we wish to respect ourselves we should stop using the term, "Hebrew," in relation to any free person among us.

Indeed, regarding the name of the language, if we had a historic source, a language that the ancient Hebrew nation spoke, then perhaps we could call it "Hebrew." And yet, I have not found a single historic evidence that this ancient nation spoke this language.

For this reason, we should consider the Talmudic literature, which is closer to the source than we are by fifteen centuries. Among them, it was unequivocally accepted that the ancient Hebrews did not use this language at all. They said, "In the beginning the Torah was given to Israel in Hebrew letters and the holy language. It was given to them once more in the days of Ezra, in Assyrian letters and the Aramaic language. Israel had sorted out for themselves the Assyrian letters and the holy language, and left the uneducated with the Hebrew letters and Aramaic language" (Sanhedrin, 21b). Thus, we learn from their words that only the letters have come to us from the Hebrews, but not the language, because they said, "Assyrian letters and the holy language" and not "Hebrew letters and language."

We do find (*Megillah*, p 8), "Conversely, a Bible that is written in translation, and a translation that is written as the Bible, and the Hebrew letters do not defile the hands." Thus, they emphasized, "translation that is written as the Bible, and Hebrew letters." They are not saying, "Translation that is written in Hebrew, and a Hebrew letters," as does the Mishnah (*Yadaim*, 4:5). This "conversely" is taken from there in order to teach us that only the letters are attributed to the Hebrews, and not the language.

Also, there is no evidence from the words of the Mishnah because it seems that here there was Roman influence on the text. But when they were memorizing the Mishnah, they made the proper precisions.

Conversely, we find that several times the Tanaim referred to the language as "the holy language." One was (*Books of Blessing*, 13), "All who dwell in the land of Israel, reads the *Shema* reading morning and evening, and speaks the holy language, merits the next world." Also, (*Shekalim*, end of Chapter 3), "We learn from Rabbi Meir that all who is permanently in the land of Israel and speaks the holy language..." etc.

Even if we assume that we can find some historic source that the ancient Hebrews spoke this language, it does not obligate us to name this language after them, since there is no trace of this nation among the living. As we have said, this name does not add to our national dignity, and only our enemies have attached it to us on purpose, to discard and slight the image of the nation's assets. Hence, we should also avoid following the English language, which calls the nation "Jews," and the language "Hebrew."

We should also determine which name suits us best: "Jews" or "Israelis." The name, "Israel," stems from our father, Jacob, who, as is written, is named as an expression of power and honor: "Your name shall no longer be called Jacob, but Israel; for you have striven with God and with men and you have prevailed" (Genesis, 32:29). It is after him that we are called "Israel."

However, after King Solomon, the nation split in two: the ten tribes, which ordained Jeroboam son of Nebat, and the two tribes, Judah and Benjamin, which remained under the kingship of Rehoboam, son of Solomon. The name, "Israel," remained with the ten tribes, and the two tribes, Judah and Benjamin, took for themselves the name, "Jews," as we have found in the story of Ester: "There was a certain Jew in Shushan the castle, whose name was Mordecai the son of Jair the son of Shimei the son of Kish, a Benjamite." Thus, the tribe of Benjamin also called themselves "Jews."

The ten tribes were exiled from the land long before the exile of Judah, and since then there has been no trace of them. The exile of Judah, who were exiled to Babylon, returned to the land after seventy years of exile and rebuilt the land. This is why throughout the period of the Second Temple, the name "Jews" is mentioned most often, and the name "Israel," is mentioned only rarely, under extraordinary circumstances.

We, the offspring of the exile of the Second Temple, are also called primarily by the name, "Jews," since we are from the exile of the Second Temple, the offspring of the two tribes, Judah and Benjamin, who have given themselves the name, "Jews." Accordingly, we should determine that the name of our nation is "Jews" and not "the Israeli nation" or "Israel," which is the name of the ten tribes.

And concerning the language, we should certainly choose the "Jewish language," and not the "Israeli language," for we do not find in the Bible this construct state of "Israeli language," as opposed to the mentioning of "Jewish": "they did not know how to speak Jewish" (Nehemia, 13:24), and also, "And God said ... 'speak now to your servants in Aramaic, for we understand it; and do not speak with us in Jewish in the ears of the people who are on the wall'" (2 Kings, 18).

Rather, we should stress that this is why they called their language, "Jewish," since the people of King Hezekiah were called "Jews," as well as those who came from the exile in Babylon. But the ten tribes, which were called "Israelis," also called their language "Israeli language." And yet, even if we assume that it is so, it is still no reason for us, the offspring of Judah and Benjamin, to call our language "Israeli."

To summarize what we have said, both the nation and the language must be given only the name Judah. The nation should be named "Jews," and the language, "Jewish." This jargon language should be called "Yiddish." Only the land may be called "the land of Israel," as it is the inheritance of all the tribes.

CRITIQUE OF MARXISM IN LIGHT OF THE NEW REALITY, AND A SOLUTION TO THE QUESTION REGARDING THE UNIFICATION OF ALL THE FACTIONS OF THE NATION

I have been asked to offer a solution, according to my view, regarding the painful problem of uniting all the parties and factions around a uniform background. At the outset, I must admit that I have no solution to this question in the way it was presented. Nor will there ever be a solution to it, as wise men from all the nations and throughout the ages have probed it but have not found a natural solution that is accepted by all the factions among them. Many have suffered, and many will suffer still before they find the golden path that does not contradict the views among them.

The difficulty of the matter is that men cannot relinquish their ideals at all, since one can make concessions when it comes to one's material life, to the extent that it is necessary for one's physical existence, but it is not so with ideals. By nature, idealists will give all that they have for the triumph of their idea. And if they must relinquish their ideals even a little, it is not an honest concession. Rather, they stay alert and wait for a time when they can reclaim what is theirs. Therefore, such compromises cannot be trusted.

It is even more so with an ancient nation, with a civilization that is thousands of years old. Its ideals have already developed in it far more than in nations that have developed more recently, so there is no hope whatsoever that they will be able to compromise on this, not even a little. It is unwise to think that in the end, the more just idea will win over the other ideas, since over time they are all right, for "there is not a man without his place, nor a matter without an hour," as our sages have stated.

For this reason, ideals keep reappearing. Ideals that were ruled out in ancient times reappeared in the Middle Ages, and once they were ruled out in the Middle Ages, they have been revived in our generation. This indicates that they are all correct, and none of them is everlasting.

But although the nations of the world suffer terribly from this racket, they still have a strong backbone that allows them to tolerate this terrible burden. Somehow it does not immediately threaten their existence. But what can a poor nation do when its entire existence depends on the crumbs and leftover food that the nations throw to them by their mercy once they are fully satiated? Their back is too frail to carry the burden of this racket, especially in this fateful time when we are standing on the very edge of the abyss—it is not a time for vanity, disputes, and internal war among brothers.

In light of the gravity of the hour, I have a genuine solution to suggest, which I believe merits acceptance, and which will unite all the factions among us into a single unit. However, before I begin to present my suggestion, I would like to put the minds of the readers at rest concerning my political views.

I must admit that I see the socialistic idea of equal and just division as the truest. Our planet is rich enough to provide for all of us, so why should we fight this tragic war to the death, which has been dimming our lives for generations? Let us share among us the labor and its produce equally, and the end to all the troubles! After all, what pleasure do even the millionaires among us derive from their possessions if not the security of their sustenance for them and for their progeny several generations on? But in a regime of just division they will also have the same certainty and even more.

And should you say that they will not have the respect that they had while they were property owners, that, too, is nothing, for all those strong ones who have gained the power to earn respect as property owners will certainly find the same amount of honor elsewhere, for the gates of competition will never be locked.

Indeed, as truthful as this ideal might be, I do not promise its adherents even a shred of paradise. Quite the contrary, they are guaranteed to have troubles as in hell, as the living proof of Russia has already taught us. However, this does not negate the correctness of this ideal.

Its only fault is that to us it is unripe. In other words, our generation is not yet morally ready to accept this government of just and equal division. This is so because we have not had enough time to evolve sufficiently to accept the motto, "from each according to his skills, to each according to his needs."

This is like the sin of *Adam ha Rishon* (the First Man). Our ancient sages have explained that the sin was because he "ate fruit unripe," before it had ripened sufficiently. For that tiny misdeed the entire world was sentenced to death. This teaches us that this is the ancestor of every detriment in the world.

People do not know how to mind and watch every thing to see if it has ripened sufficiently. Although the content of a matter may be advantageous, we must still delve more deeply to see if it is ripe, and if the receivers have grown sufficiently to digest it in their intestines. While they are still developing, the truthful and salutary will be turned to harmful and deceitful in their intestines. Thus, they are doomed to perish, for he who eats unripe fruit dies for his sin.

In light of this, the Russian entanglement has not proven that the socialist ideal is essentially unjust, as they still need time to accept this truth and justice. They are still unqualified to behave accordingly; they are only harmed by their own insufficient development and lack of aptitude for this ideal.

It is worthwhile to lend the ear to the words of M. Botkovsky (*Davar*, issue no. 4507). He asks, "Why would a politician, a member of the socialist movement, not do as that physicist, who—when faced with impairments in the interpretation he was accustomed to in the iron laws of his theory—did not deter from abandoning it? First, he gently tried to mend it, and finally, when he could no longer face reality, he was prepared to cast it off."

He explains: "In a time of ruin of the international Labor Movement, we must wash away prejudice. When facts speak the language of defeat, we must sit at the desk once more and vigorously examine the way and its principles. We must responsibly recognize the burden on the shoulders of those who carry on.

"Thus is the way of scientific thought when cornered by contradictions between the new reality and the theory that explained the old reality. Only an ideological breakthrough enables a new science, and a new life."

He concludes: "If we do not renounce our conscience, we will declare that the time has come for a fundamental debate, a time of labor pains. Now is the time for the leaders of the movement to stand up and answer the question: 'What does socialism mean today? What is the way by which the corps must go?'"

I doubt if anyone in the movement will answer his words, or perhaps be able to understand his words as they truly are. It is not easy for a hundred-year-old man who has been so successful in his studies thus far to get up and all at once strike a line through his past theory, sit at the desk, and resume his studies like that physicist, as comrade Botkovsky requires of the leaders of the socialist movement.

Yet, how do you ignore his words? While it is still possible to sit idly regarding the ruin of the international Labor Movement, since they are not facing immediate destruction, they are still secured a measure of life of submissive servants and slaves; it is not so concerning the danger that the Hebrew Labor Movement faces. They are truly facing annihilation under the slogan of the enemy "to destroy, to slay, and to cause to perish...little children and women," as during the time of Queen Esther.

We must not compare our state of ruin with the ruin of the movement among the nations of the world. If we were only sold to slavery and servitude, we would keep still, as they do. Yet we are denied even the security of the life of slaves.

Thus, we must not let the moment pass. We must attend school once more, reexamine the socialist ideal in light of the facts and contradictions that have surfaced in our days, and not fear of breaking ideological fences, for nothing stands in the way of saving lives.

For this purpose, we shall briefly review the evolution of socialism from its earliest stages. In general, there are three eras: The first was humanistic socialism based on the development of morality. It was aimed solely at the exploiters.

The second was based on the recognition of the just and evil. It was aimed primarily at the exploited, to bring them to realize that the workers are the true owners of the work, and that the produce of society belongs to them. Since the workers are the majority in society, they were certain that once they realized that they are the just, they would rise as one, take what is theirs, and establish a government of just and equal division in society.

The third is Marxism, which succeeded more than all of them, and which is based on Historic Materialism. The great contradiction between the creative-forces, which are the workers, and the ones who exploit them, the employers, necessitates that society will ultimately come to peril and destruction. Then the revolution will come in production and distribution. The capitalistic government would be forced into ruin in favor of the government of the proletariat.

In his view, this government was to emerge by itself, by way of cause and consequence. But in order to bring the end sooner still, counsels must be sought, and obstacles must be placed before the bourgeois government, to bring the revolution sooner.

Before I come to criticize his method, I must admit his method is the most just of all its predecessors. After all, we are witnessing the great success it had in quantity and quality throughout the world before it came to practical experimentation among the many millions in Russia. Until then, almost all the leaders of humanity were drawn to it, and this is a true testimony to the justness of his method.

Besides, even theoretically, his words have merit, and no one has been able to contradict his historic stance that humanity is headed slowly and gradually upward, as if on a ladder. Each step is but the negation of its former, hence each movement and phase that humanity has taken in the political government is but a repudiation of its preceding state.

The duration of every political phase is just the time it takes to unveil its shortcomings and evil. While discovering its faults, it makes way for a new phase, liberated from these failings. Thus, these impairments that appear in a situation and destroy it are the very forces of human evolution, as they raise humanity to a more corrected state.

In addition, the faults in the next phase bring humanity to a third and better state. Thus, persisting successively, these negative forces that appear in the situations are the reasons for the progress of humanity. Through them, it climbs up the rungs of the ladder. They are reliable in performing their duty, which is to bring humankind to the last, most desirable state of evolution, purified of any ignominy and blemish.

In this historic process, he shows us how the feudal government manifested its shortcomings and was ruined, making way for the bourgeois government. Now it is time for the bourgeois government to show its faults and be ruined, making way for the better still governance, which according to him, is the government of the proletariat.

However, in this last point, where he promises us that after the ruin of the current bourgeois government, a proletariat government will immediately be instated, here is the flaw in his method: The new reality before us denies it. He thought that the proletariat governance would be the subsequent step to the bourgeois governance, and hence determined that by negating the bourgeois government, a proletariat one would be established instantly. Yet, reality proves that the step following the ruin of the present government is that of Nazis or Fascists.

Evidently, we are still in the middle stages of human development. Humanity has not yet reached the highest level of the ladder of evolution. Who can assume how many rivers of blood are yet to be shed before humankind reaches the desired level?

In order to find a way out of this complication, we must thoroughly perceive the above-mentioned gradual law of evolution upon which he based his entire method. We should know that this law is inclusive for the entire creation; all of nature's systems are based on it, organic and inorganic alike, up to the human species with all its idealistic properties, as well as the materials.

In all the above, there is none that does not obey the iron law of gradual evolution resulting from the collision of these two forces with one another: 1) a positive force, meaning constructive, and 2) a negative force, meaning negative and destructive.

They create and complement the entire reality, in general and particular, through their harsh and perpetual war with one another. As we have said above, the negative force appears at the end of every political phase, elevating it to a better state. Thus, the phases follow one another until they reach their ultimate perfection.

Let us take planet Earth as an example: First, it was but a ball of fog-like gas. Through the gravity inside it, over time, it concentrated the atoms in it into a closer circle. As a result, the ball of gas became a liquid ball of fire.

Over eons of terrible wars between the two forces in Earth, the positive and the negative, the chilling force in it was finally triumphant over the force of liquid fire. It cooled a thin crust around the Earth and hardened there.

However, the planet had not yet grown still from the war between the forces, and after some time the liquid force of fire overpowered and erupted in great tumult from the bowels of the Earth, rising and shattering the cold, hard crust to pieces, turning the planet back into a liquid ball of fire. Then an era of new wars began until the cool force overpowered the force of fire once more, and a second crust was chilled around the ball, harder, thicker, and more durable against the outbreak of the fluids from amidst the ball.

This time it lasted longer, but at last, the liquid forces overpowered once again and erupted from the bowels of the Earth, breaking the crust in pieces. Once more, everything was ruined and became a liquid ball.

Thus, the eons interchanged, and each time the cooling force prevailed, the crust it made grew thicker. Finally, the positive forces overpowered the negative ones and came into complete harmony: The liquids took their place in the bowels of the Earth, and the cold crust became thick enough around them to enable the creation of organic life atop it, as it is today.

All organic bodies develop by the same order. From the moment they are planted to the end of their ripening, they undergo several hundred periods of situations due to the two forces, the positive and the negative, and their war against each other, as described regarding the Earth. These wars yield the ripening of the fruit.

Also, every living thing begins with a tiny drop of fluid. Through gradual development over several hundred phases through the above-mentioned struggle of forces, it finally becomes "A big ox, fit for every work," or "A great man, fit for all his roles."

However, there should be yet another distinction between the ox and the human: Today, the ox has already reached its final phase of development. For us, however, the material force is yet insufficient to bring us to completion due to the contemplative power in us, which is thousands of times more valuable than the material force in us. Thus, for humans there is a new order of gradual development, unlike any other animal: the gradual development of human thought.

Also, being a social creature, the individual development is not enough. Rather, one's final perfection depends on the development of all the members of society. With respect to the development of one's intellectual capability, namely the ability to discern what is good and what is bad for him—though we must not think that man is still at the stage of a primitive man—it is clear that we have not reached perfection. Rather, we are still in the midst of our development, still given to the war between the positive and negative forces, as was said above regarding Earth—which are faithful messengers to their role of bringing humanity to its final completion.

As I have said, since the socialistic ideal is the most just of all the methods, it requires a highly developed generation that can process it and behave accordingly. Since today's humanity is in the middle rungs of the ladder of development, still in the midst of the conflict between the positive and negative forces, it is as yet unfit for this sublime idea. Rather, it is premature in it, like an unripe fruit. Hence, not only is it foul tasting, but the negative force in it is also harmful, sometimes deadly venom. This is the trouble of that nation, for which it suffers so, as they are premature and lack the elementary qualities suitable for assumption of this just governance.

The reader must not suspect that I have any spiritual concept on this matter, for Marx himself says the same thing: He admits that "on the first level of society, deficiencies are unavoidable." However, he promises that "on the highest level of the cooperative society, once the crass hierarchy of people in the division of the work has disappeared, along with the contradiction between physical work and spiritual work, when work itself becomes a necessity and not a means of provision, when along with the multifaceted development of the personality, production forces will grow and all of society's fountains will flow abundantly, then the narrow bourgeois perspective will vanish and society will write upon its banner: 'From each according to his ability, to each .

according to his needs." (Due to the pertinence of the words to our discussion, I have copied his excerpt in full.)

Thus, he, too, admits that it is hopeless to wait for completely just governance before humanity achieves the highest level, before work itself becomes a vital need, meaning life's principle, and not for the purpose of provision. However, he determines that while society is at a lower level, it should also be conducted by cooperative governance, for all its flaws.

But as was said above, this is the drawback in his method. Soviet Russia has already proven that an insufficiently developed society will invert the cooperative governance into the worst governance in the world. Moreover, he assumed that the subsequent phase to the ruin of today's governance is the governance of the workers, but reality has shown that the subsequent governance to today's governance is the Nazi or fascistic governance. This is a grave error. And worst of all, its completion, by and large, threatens specifically the Jewish nation, without any differentiation of class.

We should indeed learn from history. First arises the question: Such a supervisor who has shaken the world with his method, how did he make such a grave mistake? What is the obstacle that tripped him? Indeed, this mandates serious and meticulous consideration of his words.

As was said above, he based his method on historic materialism—that society develops through its conflicting forces by way of cause and consequence, from state to state. When the negative force prevails, it ruins the state, and a better state emerges in its stead through the positive force. They continue to fight until eventually the positive force appears in full.

However, this means that the perfection of society is guaranteed by default, since the negative force will not leave it before it brings it to completion. It follows that we can sit idly and wait for the anticipated self-development. So why all this trouble of this tactic he had placed upon us?

Indeed, it is a silly question, for this is the whole difference between man and beast: All animals rely entirely on nature. They are utterly unable to promote nature or help themselves without it. Not so with man. He is endowed with intellectual powers by which he becomes free of the shackles of nature and promotes it. His way is to emulate nature's work and do likewise. He does not wait for the fledglings to hatch naturally, for the hen to come and warm the eggs. Rather, he builds for himself a machine that warms the eggs and hatches the chicks, like the natural hen.

And if he does this in specific things, he will certainly do it with regard to the development of the whole of humanity. He will not rely on the conflicting forces, with him becoming an object in their collisions. Rather, he will advance nature and will thoroughly emulate its work in this development. He will arrange for himself a good and convenient tactic to bring about the happy end in less time and with less suffering.

This is what Marx wanted by his tactic: the organization, the Class Conflicts, and placing hurdles to undermine the capitalistic regime. His tactic would ease the pains of the suffering subjects, and the stomping on their backs. It would invigorate them to be their own subjects, and rush the end of the backward regime to make room for the happy rule of the proletariat. In a word, the Marxist tactic turns the objects into subjects, establishing for them development as they wish.

Summary: The basis is the nature of human development through causal connection, which we see as a natural machine for development. The tactic is a kind of artificial machine for human development, similar to the natural machine. The benefit from the tactic is saving time and diminishing agony.

Now we can begin the critique of his method in a simple manner. It is clear that when we want to make a machine that replaces nature's work, we first need to closely observe nature's mechanism. Subsequently, we can set up an artificial mechanism similar to the natural machine.

For example, if we want to make a machine that replaces a hen's belly, which warms the eggs and hatches the chicks, we must first thoroughly understand nature's forces and manners of development, which operate in the hen's belly. We observe them and make a machine similar to a hen's belly, which can hatch chicks likewise.

It is likewise concerning our matter. When we want to make a machine that will replace the machine of natural human development, here, too, we must first examine those two forces—positive and negative—that operate in nature. It is a machine by which nature performs the procedure of development. Then we, too, will know how to establish a tactic that is similar to the mechanism of nature's natural machine of development, and which will be just as successful in developing humanity. Clearly, if we misunderstand the mechanism of the natural machine, our substitute will be useless, since the whole idea here is to mimic natural ways of creation and adapt artificial ones in their stead.

To be original, to define the matters in terms that will prevent any mistakes by any party, we should define the two forces—positive and negative—operating in the machine of human development by two names: "egoism" and "altruism."

I am not referring to the moral terms regarding them, which we ordinarily use. Rather, only to the material aspect of them, meaning the extent to which they are rooted in man's body to the point that one can no longer liberate oneself from them. That is, with respect to their being active forces in a person: 1) The egoistic force functions in a person similar to centripetal rays [a force that aims toward the center in a circular motion], drawing them from outside the person, and they gather within the body itself. 2) The altruistic serves as centrifugal rays [a force directing outward in a circular motion], which flow from within the body outward.

These forces exist in all parts of reality, in each according to its essence. They also exist in man, according to his essence. They are the key factors in all our actions. There are facts that are caused by a force that serves for one's own individual existence. This is like a force that draws from the external reality to the center of the body anything that is beneficial to itself. Were it not for this force, which serves one, the object itself would not exist. This is called "egoism."

Conversely, there are facts that are caused by a force that flows toward benefiting bodies outside of itself. This force works to benefit others, and it can be called "altruism."

By these distinctions, I name the two forces that struggle with one another on the path of human development. I shall call the positive force, an "altruistic force," and I shall call the negative force, an "egoistic force."

By the term, "egoism," I am not referring to the original egoism. Rather, I am referring to "narrow egoism." That is, the original egoism is nothing but self-love, which is all of one's positive, individualistic power of existence. In that respect, it is not at odds with the altruistic force, although it does not serve it.

However, it is the nature of egoism that the manner of using it makes it very narrow, since it is more or less compelled to acquire a nature of hatred and exploitation of others in order to make one's own existence easier. Also, it is not abstract hatred, but one that appears in acts of abusing one's friend for one's own benefit, growing murkier according to its degrees, such as deceiving, stealing, robbing, and murdering. This is called "narrow egoism," and in that respect it is at odds with—and the complete opposite from—love of others. It is a negative force that destroys the society.

Its opposite is the altruistic force. This is society's constructive force, since all that one does for another is done only by the altruistic force, as said above. Also, it ascends in its degrees: 1) The first facts of this constructive force are having children and family life. 2) The second ones are benefiting relatives. 3) The third is benefiting the state, 4) and the fourth is to benefit the entire world.

The whole cause of the social structuring is the altruistic force. As said above, these are the elements that operate in the natural machine of the development of humanity— the egoistic force, which is negative to society, and the altruistic, positive force, which is positive for society.

In his emulation of the natural machine of development, Marx regarded only the results of these negative and positive forces, which are the construction and destruction that take place in society. He established the plan of his tactic according to them, and overlooked what causes these results.

This is similar to a physician not noticing the root cause of an illness, but healing the patient only according to its superficial symptoms. This method always does more harm than good, since you must take both into account: the cause of the illness and the illness itself, and then you can prescribe a successful remedy. That same deficiency exists in the Marxist tactic: He did not take into account the subjective forces in society, but only the constructive and the flaws.

As a result, the direction of his tactic was opposite from the purposeful direction, for while the purposeful direction is altruistic, the direction of the tactic was to the contrary. It is clear that the cooperative governance must be conducted in an altruistic direction, since the very words, "just division," contain a pure altruistic perception, and is completely devoid of the framework of egoism.

Egoism strives to use the other entirely for oneself. For itself, there is no justice in reality whatsoever, as long as it is not working for its own good. The very word, "justice," means "mutual, fair relations," which is a concept in favor of the other. And to the same extent that it acknowledges the entitlement of the other, it necessarily loses its own egoistic entitlement.

It turns out that the very term, "just division," is an altruistic one. Factually speaking, it is impossible to mend the rifts that arise in society with just division, unless by exaggerated altruism. It is so because the reward for spiritual work is greater than that of physical work, and the work of the nimble is more rewarding than the work of the slow, and a bachelor should receive less than one who has a family. Also, the work hours should be equal to all, and the produce of the work should be equal to all. Indeed, how do we mend these rifts?

These are the main rifts, but they split into myriad other rifts, as it appears before us in the Soviet play. The only way to patch them is through a good altruistic will, where the spiritual workers relinquish some of their share in favor of the physical workers, and the bachelors in favor of the married ... or as Marx himself put it, "The work itself will become an imperative need and not merely a means of provision." This is nothing short of a complete altruistic direction.

And since the purposeful regime must be in the altruistic nature, it is necessary that the tactic that aims toward that goal should also be in the same direction as the goal, namely an altruistic direction.

However, in the Marxist tactic, we find the narrowest egoistic direction. This is the opposite direction from the goal: the nurturing of hatred of the opposite class, placing hurdles and ruining the old regime, and cultivating among the workers a feeling that the whole world is enjoying on the back of their work. All these overly intensify the narrow egoistic forces among the workers. It completely deprives them of the altruistic force inherent in them by nature. And if the tactic is in the opposite direction to the goal, how will one ever reach it?

This engendered the contradiction between his theory and the new reality: He thought that the subsequent stage to the bourgeois regime would be a cooperative workers' regime, but in the end we are living witnesses that if the democratic bourgeois government were to be ruined now, a Nazi and fascist regime would promptly rise in its stead. Also, it will not necessarily be through the current war, but whenever the democratic government is ruined, a fascist, Nazi regime will inherit it.

There is no doubt that if this were to happen, the workers would be pushed back a thousand years. They will have to wait for several regimes to arise by cause and consequence before the world returns to today's democratic bourgeois regime. All this emerged out of the egoistic tactic that was given to those subjects that should be the workers' governance, and led the movement in an opposite direction from the goal.

We should also take into account that all those who are ruining the natural process of the just governance actually came from the proletariat and emerged from their midst, and not necessarily the Soviets, but the majority of Nazis were also initially pure socialists, as well as the majority of fascists. Even Mussolini himself was initially an enthusiastic socialist leader. This completes the picture, how the Marxist tactic has led the workers in the complete opposite direction from the goal.

Indeed, it is difficult to determine that such a straightforward matter will be overlooked by the creator of the Marxist method, especially since he himself determined that "There is no remedy for the cooperative society before the crass hierarchy in division of work and conflicts between physical work and spiritual work disappears." Thus, it is clear that he was aware that a cooperative society without the members' complete relinquishment of their shares in favor of the fellow person is unsustainable.

And since he knew of that altruistic element that is mandatory in society, I say that he did not intend at all to offer us a purposeful procedure by his tactic. Rather, he intended primarily to hurry—through this tactic—the end of the present unjust governance, on the one hand, and on the other hand, to organize the international proletariat and prepare them to be a strong, decisive force when the bourgeois regime is ruined. These are two necessary fundamentals in the stages that facilitate the regime of a cooperative society.

In that respect, his tactic is a genius invention, the like of which we do not find in history. And concerning the establishing of the happy society, he relied on history itself to complete it, for it was clear to him that in dire times, when the bourgeois regime begins to die, the proletariat organization will find itself unprepared to assume governance. At that time the workers will have to choose one of two options: 1) either to destroy themselves and let the true destructors, the Nazis and the fascists, take over the helm of governance, or 2) find a good tactic by which to qualify the workers to assume governance into their own hands.

In his mind, he was certain that when we come to a state where the international proletariat joins into a decisive power in the world, we will thank him for the validity of his method, which has brought us thus far, and we ourselves will seek the way to continue moving toward the goal. Indeed, there has never been an inventor who did not leave the completion of his work to his successors.

If we look deeper into his method we will see that, in fact, he could not invent for us the tactic to complete the qualification of the workers, as they are two procedures that contradict one another. To create the fastest movement and annihilate the governances of abusers, he had to use the procedure in the direction of the narrowest egoism, meaning to develop profound hatred to the class of abusers in order to increase the negative power into an instrument that can destroy the old regime in the quickest possible time, and to organize the workers in the strongest ties.

For this reason, he had to uproot and neutralize the altruistic force in the proletariat, whose nature is to tolerate and concede to its abusers. To qualify the workers in "practical socialism," so they could assume the governance *de facto*, he had to use the procedure in the altruistic direction, which contradicts the "organizational procedure." Thus, he must have left this work for us on purpose.

He did not doubt our understanding or ability since the matter was so straightforward that a cooperative government is feasible only on an altruistic basis, so we would have to adopt a new tactic in the altruistic direction and qualify the workers to take governance into their hands in a practical and sustainable manner. However, to comment on it, he found it necessary to depict for us the form of just governance of the proletariat in the abbreviated words, "Society will make its motto, 'From each according to his skills, to each according to his work.'" Thus, even a totally blind person would find these words to mean that just governance is inconceivable if not in an altruistic society in the full sense of the word.

From that perspective, Marxism did not encounter any confrontation due to the unsuccessful Russian experiment. And if Marxism has been stopped, it is only because its role in the first act has been completed, namely organizing the international proletariat into a force. Now we must find a practical way to qualify the movement to actually assume the government into its hands.

As said above, the current procedure must be in the completely opposite direction from the previous tactic. Where we had cultivated excessive egoism, which was very successful in the first act, we must now cultivate excessive altruism among the workers. This is utterly mandatory for the social nature of the cooperative regime. Thus, we will lead the movement with confidence to its practical role of assuming governance into its own hands in its final, happy form.

I know that it is not the easiest work to completely reverse the direction of the movement so that all who hear it will be burned by it as if by boiling water. Yet, it is not as bad as it is portrayed. We can bring the movement into recognition through proper explanation that the interest of the class depends on this, "whether it persists or perishes," whether to continue the Marxist movement or hand over the reigns of governance to the Nazis and the fascists—the most dangerous forces to the government of the workers, which pose the risk of regression by a thousand years.

When the masses understand this, it is certain that they will easily adopt the new, practical tactic leading them to actual assumption of the governance. Who does not remember how the whole world anxiously awaited the successful end of the Soviet regime? And were they not successful, the whole world would undoubtedly be under the reins of the cooperative government. Indeed, the Russians could not possibly succeed because the organizational direction to which the masses are accustomed is the egoistic one, which is necessary in the first act, and by nature, it is a power that destroys the cooperative governance.

Before the method is accepted, it is too soon to speak in detail about the practical program of this direction, especially since the essay has become too long already. Briefly, we can say that we must set up such dissemination, scientifically and practically, that will be certain to install in the public opinion that any member who does not excel in altruism is like a predator that is unfit to be among humans, until one feels oneself within the society as a murderer and a robber.

If we systematically engage in circulating this matter using the appropriate manners, it will not require such a long process. Hitlerism proves that within a short period of time, an entire country has been turned upside down through propaganda and accepted his bizarre notion.

Now that historic facts have clarified the right way in which the movement should go henceforth, I urgently appeal to our workers. As was said above, the nations of the world may wait, especially now that there is global upheaval and we must first be rid of the Hitlerian danger. But we have no time to waste. I ask that you will promptly pay attention to this new method that I have proposed, and which I call "practical socialism," for until now the role of socialism, in my view, was merely "organizational socialism," as said above.

If my method is accepted, we should also change the outward tactic, where instead of the old weapon of class hatred and hatred of religion, they will be given a new weapon of hatred of the excessive egoism in the proprietors. It is successful for its task from every angle because not only will the opposite class be unable to defend using the thick shields of moral and religious dogmas, it will also uproot along the way various noxious weeds of Nazism and fascism that have taken root quite strongly among the proletariat itself, risking its existence, as above said.

We should also take into account the beauty of this weapon, which is most enticing and can unite our youth around it. In fact, the change is not so much in the tactic, but only in the result. Until now, when they fought against the depriving of the class, the fighter always looks through the narrow possessive-egoistic perspective, as he is protecting his own possession. Thus, along with his war, the excessive egoistic force increases in him, and the warriors themselves are caught up in the same bourgeois perspective.

It is also very unlike the proprietors' approach, for they believe they have complete entitlement from all sides, by law, religion, and ethics, protecting themselves by all the means. However, when fighting against the egoism of the proprietors using the broad perspective of an altruistic perception, the result is that the power of altruism grows within them in proportion to the level of their struggle. Thus, the entitlement of the proprietors becomes very flawed and they cannot defend themselves, for this type of war relies heavily on the ethical and religious perception in the proprietors themselves.

Thus, my method holds the basis for national unity, for which we are so thirsty at this time. Presumably, history itself has already broken many of the political partitions among us, for now we can no longer distinguish between non-Zionists, spiritual Zionists, political Zionists, territorial ones, etc. Now that all the hopes of breathing free air outside our country have been shattered, even the most devout non-Zionists have become, by necessity, complete practical Zionists. Thus, in principle, the majority of rifts among us have been mended.

However, we are still suffering from two terrible partitions: 1) class partition; 2) religious partition. We must not slight these whatsoever, nor can we hope to ever be rid of them. However, if my new method of "practical socialism," which I have suggested, is accepted by the movement, we will be rid once and for all of the class wedge, too, which has been stuck in the nation's back.

As was said above, the new tactic takes much from religion, and does not aim at the abusing sinners, but only at their sins—only at the contemptible egoism within them. In truth, that same war will unfold in part within the movement, too, which will necessarily abolish class hatred and religious hatred. We will obtain the ability to understand one another and achieve complete unity of the nation with all its factions and parties, as this perilous time for all of us requires. This is the guarantee to our victory on all fronts.

REGARDING THE QUESTION
OF THE DAY

We have grown weary of the contradicting pieces of information regarding Italy's joining the war that we receive each day. Once, we are promised that Mussolini would not dare to fight the Allies, and once, that he is promptly joining the war. Changes occur daily, and nerves are wrecked. All indications show that all these pieces of information are edited and presented to us by a Hitler-Mussolini factory, whose only aim is to weaken our nerves.

One way or the other, we must seek shelter from them. We must promptly turn away from all these odd pieces of news and try to follow the leading factors and all of these adventures by ourselves, so we might understand from them all those perplexing moves of Hitler-Mussolini.

But mainly, we should note the contract of their agreement. It is known that they have signed two contracts: The first was merely a political agreement, which they named the "Rome-Berlin Axis." Its content is mutual political aid and division of certain areas of influence between them. Following this agreement, Hitler provided political aid to Mussolini in his war in Ethiopia, and Mussolini did likewise for Hitler in his prewar adventures, and continues to do it still. 2) Near the outbreak of the war, they made a second, military pact, whose content we do not know. However, in general, we know that they have committed to actual mutual military aid.

There is sufficient proof to assume that they did not commit to wage the war together promptly, as with the England-France agreement. This agreement was built entirely on Hitler's initiative, for with it he wished to secure himself from any trouble that might come—should he be in military crisis and will need Italy's assistance. At such a time, the agreement commits Italy to come to his aid, following Hitler's invitation, and naturally, under certain conditions regarding the division of the spoil.

But essentially, Hitler did not think that he would need Italy's military assistance. There were two reasons for it: 1) He was confident of his strength and did not trust Italy's military skills. 2) The previous political agreement, too, the "Rome-Berlin Axis," already secured him substantial military aid, since by mere political maneuvers Italy could occupy many of his enemies' forces on the borders of Italy. This is not far from taking an active role in the war. Thus, he had no desire at all to actually include Mussolini in his war.

The military pact that he had made with him was only in case of a military crisis, which would commit Mussolini to come to his aid explicitly following Hitler's invitation, and the initiative would not be in Mussolini's hands at all.

Correspondingly, Mussolini was hoping to fulfill through this war all of his fascist plans to reinstate the ancient Roman Empire. He could not have hoped for a better opportunity than to fight his war alongside Hitler. Undoubtedly, he is anxious for the moment when Hitler asks him to join him in the war. Presumably, Hitler has not lost faith in his power and as yet has no desire whatsoever to include him in the war, or put differently, to share the spoil with him.

It therefore follows that as long as we do not feel that there is a real crisis among Hitler's armies, we have nothing to fear from Mussolini's threats and his preparations for the war. These are nothing but shrewd military maneuvers intended to stall the Allies on his borders and weaken the power of the Allies in the front as much as possible, in accord with the conditions of the "Rome-Berlin Axis" contract. (While writing, information has arrived that Italy has joined the war, so the essay was stopped midway. We will finish the article according to the present reality.)

Now that Italy's joining the war has become a fact, much has been clarified, if we discuss according to the line we have depicted. Now we know for certain that in the last battle, Hitler has come to a real crisis and his powers have been completely worn there. Otherwise, there is no doubt that he would not include Italy in the war. For this reason, Italy's joining the war is good news, of sorts, concerning German's downfall. We hope that Italy's assistance will not save it, too, and now the victory of the Allies is more certain than ever.

PUBLIC STAGE

We hereby offer room in our paper for a "public stage" for anyone who discusses national matters, and especially the unification of the nation. Also, anyone with an important national matter, or a plan to unite the nation, as well as arguments that scrutinize these matters—we are willing to take them and publish them in our paper.

The Editors

Detailed Table of Contents

Editor's Note 7

The Writings of the Last Generation 9

Introduction to the Writings of the Last Generation .. 11

Part One 15

The Positive 30

The Negative 37

Debate 45

News 48

Appendices and Drafts 51

Section One 51

Section Two 55

Section Three 57

Section Four 58

Section Five 59

Section Six 60

Section Seven 63

Section Eight 64

Section Nine 65

Section Ten 66

Section Eleven 67

Section Twelve 73

Section Thirteen 76

Section Fourteen 77

The Differences between Me and Schopenhauer 78

Part Two..81

Leaders of the Generation.............................81

Action before Thought....................................82

Three Postulates [Axioms]..............................82

Truth and Falsehood.......................................82

Personal Opinion and Public Opinion..........83

The Corruption in Public Opinion................84

The Origin of Democracy and Socialism......84

The Contradiction between Democracy and Socialism...85

Contact with Him..85

Rebuilding the World.......................................86

Nazism Is Not an Offshoot of Germany..........88

The One Counsel..88

Nihilism..89

Materialistic Monism.......................................89

Outside of This World......................................90

What Is Outside of This World?.....................90

The Essence of Religion...................................91

The Leaders of the Public...............................92

Perception of the World...................................92

The Essence of Corruption and Correction Is in the
Public Opinion...92

Quantity vs. Quality...93

The Majority Is as Primitive as Prehistoric Man...........93

The Quickest Action Is Religion....................93

The Prodigies...93

Teleology...94

Causality and Choice.......................................95

Path of Torah..96

Good Deeds and *Mitzvot*......................................96

Life's Tendency..97

Life's Purpose...98

Two Enslavements in the World....................................99

Part Three..101

    Section One...101

    Section Two..103

Part Four..115

    Section One...115

    Section Two..117

    Section Three...119

Part Five 125

The Nation 141

    Our Intention 143

    The Individual and the Nation.............................146

    The Name of the Nation, the Language, and the Land...154

    Critique of Marxism in Light of the New Reality.........159

    Regarding the Question of the Day 183

    Public Stage..186

Detailed Table of Contents..187

Further Reading...191

Contact Information...200

Further Reading

The Secrets of the Eternal Book

The Five Books of Moses (The Torah) are part of the all-time bestselling book, The Bible. Ironically, the Bible is an encoded text. Beneath it lies another level, a hidden subtext that describes the ascent of humanity toward its highest level—the attainment of the Creator.

The Secrets of the Eternal Book decodes some of the Bible's most enigmatic, yet oft-cited epochs, such as the story of Creation, and the Children of Israel's exodus from Egypt.

The author's lively and easygoing style makes for a smooth entrance into the deepest level of reality, where one changes one's world simply by contemplation and desire.

Unlocking the Zohar

The greatest Kabbalist of the 20th century, Rav Yehuda Ashlag (1884-1954) paved a new way for us by which we can reveal the secrets of The Book of Zohar. He wrote the Sulam [Ladder] commentary and four introductions to the book, in order to help us understand the forces that govern our lives, and to teach us how we can assume control over our destinies.

Unlocking the Zohar is an invitation to a wondrous journey to a higher world. The author, Kabbalist Dr. Michael Laitman, wisely ushers us into the revelations of the Sulam commentary. In so doing, Laitman helps us fine-tune our thoughts as we read in The Zohar, to maximize the spiritual benefit derived from reading it.

Unlocking the Zohar is an invitation to a wondrous journey to a higher world. The author, Kabbalist Dr. Michael Laitman, wisely ushers us into the revelations of the Sulam commentary. In so doing, Laitman helps us fine-tune our thoughts as we read in *The Zohar*, to maximize the spiritual benefit derived from reading it.

The Kabbalah Experience

The depth of the wisdom revealed in the questions and answers within this book will inspire readers to reflect and contemplate. This is not a book to race through, but rather one that should be read thoughtfully and carefully. With this approach, readers will begin to experience a growing sense of enlightenment while simply absorbing the answers to the questions every Kabbalah student asks along the way.

The Kabbalah Experience is a guide from the past to the future, revealing situations that all students of Kabbalah will experience at some point along their journeys. For those who cherish every moment in life, this book offers unparalleled insights into the timeless wisdom of Kabbalah.

The Path of Kabbalah

This unique book combines beginners' material with more advanced concepts and teachings. If you have read a book or two of Laitman's, you will find this book very easy to relate to.

While touching upon basic concepts such as perception of reality and Freedom of Choice, *The Path of Kabbalah* goes deeper and expands beyond the scope of beginners' books. The structure of the worlds, for example, is explained in greater detail here than in the "pure" beginners' books. Also described is the spiritual root of mundane matters such as the Hebrew calendar and the holidays.

The Book of Zohar: annotations to the Ashlag commentary

The Book of Zohar is an age-old source of wisdom and the basis for all Kabbalistic literature. Since its appearance, it has been the primary, and often only source used by Kabbalists.

Written in a unique and metaphorical language, *The Book of Zohar* enriches our understanding of reality and widens our worldview. Rav Yehuda Ashlag's unique *Sulam* (Ladder) commentary allows us to grasp the hidden meanings of the text and "climb" toward the lucid perceptions and insights that the book holds for those who study it.

Attaining the Worlds Beyond

From the introduction to *Attaining the Worlds Beyond*: "...Not feeling well on the Jewish New Year's Eve of September 1991, my teacher called me to his bedside and handed me his notebook, saying, 'Take it and learn from it.' The following morning, he perished in my arms, leaving me and many of his other disciples without guidance in this world.

"He used to say, 'I want to teach you to turn to the Creator, rather than to me, because He is the only strength, the only Source of all that exists, the only one who can really help you, and He awaits your prayers for help. When you seek help in your search for freedom from the bondage of this world, help in elevating yourself above this world, help in finding the self, and help in determining your purpose in life, you must turn to the Creator, who sends you all those aspirations in order to compel you to turn to Him.'"

Attaining the Worlds Beyond holds within it the content of that notebook, as well as other inspiring texts. This book reaches out to all those seekers who want to find a logical, reliable way to understand the world we live in. This fascinating introduction to the wisdom of Kabbalah will enlighten the mind, invigorate the heart, and move readers to the depths of their souls.

The Wise Heart: Tales and allegories by three contemporary sages

Kabbalah students and enthusiasts in Kabbalah often wonder what the spiritual world actually feels like to a Kabbalist. *The Wise Heart* is a lovingly crafted anthology comprised of tales and allegories by Kabbalist Dr. Michael Laitman, his mentor, Rav Baruch Ashlag (Rabash), and Rabash's father and mentor, Rav Yehuda Ashlag, author of the acclaimed *Sulam* (Ladder) commentary on *The Book of Zohar*. The poems herein offer surprising and often amusing depictions of human nature, with a loving and tender touch that is truly unique to Kabbalists.

Shamati (I Heard)

Rav Michael Laitman's words on the book: "Among all the texts and notes that were used by my teacher, Rav Baruch Shalom Halevi Ashlag (the Rabash), there was one special notebook he always carried. This notebook contained transcripts of his conversations with his father, Rav Yehuda Leib Halevi Ashlag (Baal HaSulam), author of the *Sulam* (Ladder) commentary on *The Book of Zohar*, *The Study of the Ten Sefirot* (a commentary on the texts of the Kabbalist, Ari), and many other works on Kabbalah.

"Not feeling well on the Jewish New Year's Eve of September 1991, the Rabash summoned me to his bedside and handed me a notebook, whose cover contained only one word, *Shamati* (I Heard). As he handed the notebook, he said, 'Take it and learn from it.' The following morning, my teacher perished in my arms, leaving me and many of his other disciples without guidance in this world.

Committed to Rabash's legacy to disseminate the wisdom of Kabbalah, I published the notebook just as it was written, thus retaining the text's transforming powers. Among all the books of Kabbalah, *Shamati* is a unique and compelling creation."

Kabbalah for the Student

Kabbalah for the Student offers authentic texts by Rav Yehuda Ashlag, author of the *Sulam* (Ladder) commentary on *The Book of Zohar*, his son and successor, Rav Baruch Ashlag, as well as other great Kabbalists. It also offers illustrations that accurately depict the evolution of the Upper Worlds as Kabbalists experience them. The book also contains several explanatory essays that help us understand the texts within.

In *Kabbalah for the Student*, Rav Michael Laitman, PhD, Rav Baruch Ashlag's personal assistant and prime student, compiled all the texts a Kabbalah student would need in order to attain the spiritual worlds. In his daily lessons, Rav Laitman bases his teaching on these inspiring texts, thus helping novices and veterans alike to better understand the spiritual path we undertake on our fascinating journey to the Higher Realms.

Rabash—the Social Writings

Rav Baruch Shalom HaLevi Ashlag (Rabash) played a remarkable role in the history of Kabbalah. He provided us with the necessary final link connecting the wisdom of Kabbalah to our human experience. His father and teacher was the great Kabbalist, Rav Yehuda Leib HaLevi Ashlag, known as Baal HaSulam for his *Sulam* (Ladder) commentary on *The Book of Zohar*. Yet, if not for the essays of Rabash, his father's efforts to disclose the wisdom of Kabbalah to all would have been in vain. Without those essays, few would be able to achieve the spiritual attainment that Baal HaSulam so desperately wanted us to obtain.

The writings in this book aren't just for reading. They are more like an experiential user's guide. It is very important to work with them in order to see what they truly contain. The reader should try to put them into practice by living out the emotions Rabash so masterfully describes. He always advised his students to summarize the articles, to work with the texts, and those who attempt it discover that it always yields new insights. Thus, readers are advised to work with the texts, summarize them, translate them, and implement them in the group. Those who do so will discover the power in the writings of Rabash.

Gems of Wisdom: words of the great Kabbalists from all generations

Through the millennia, Kabbalists have bequeathed us with numerous writings. In their compositions, they have laid out a structured method that can lead, step by step, unto a world of eternity and wholeness.

Gems of Wisdom is a collection of selected excerpts from the writings of the greatest Kabbalists from all generations, with particular emphasis on the writings of Rav Yehuda Leib HaLevi Ashlag (Baal HaSulam), author of the *Sulam* [Ladder] commentary of *The Book of Zohar*.

The sections have been arranged by topics, to provide the broadest view possible on each topic. This book is a useful guide to any person desiring spiritual advancement.

Let There Be Light: selected excerpts from The Book of Zohar

The Zohar contains all the secrets of Creation, but until recently the wisdom of Kabbalah was locked under a thousand locks. Thanks to the work of Rav Yehuda Ashlag (1884-1954), the last of the great Kabbalists, *The Zohar* is revealed today in order to propel humanity to its next degree.

Let There Be Light contains selected excerpts from the series *Zohar for All*, a refined edition of *The Book of Zohar* with the *Sulam* commentary. Each piece was carefully chosen for its beauty and depth as well as its capacity to draw the reader into *The Zohar* and get the most out of the reading experience. As *The Zohar* speaks of nothing but the intricate web that connects all souls, diving into its words attracts the special force that exists in that state of oneness, where we are all connected.

The Science of Kabbalah

Kabbalist and scientist Rav Michael Laitman, PhD, designed this book to introduce readers to the special language and terminology of the authentic wisdom of Kabbalah. Here, Rav Laitman reveals authentic Kabbalah in a manner both rational and mature. Readers are gradually led to under-stand the logical design of the Universe and the life that exists in it.

The Science of Kabbalah, a revolutionary work unmatched in its clarity, depth, and appeal to the intellect, will enable readers to approach the more technical works of Baal HaSulam (Rabbi Yehuda Ashlag), such as *The Study of the Ten Sefirot* and *The Book of Zohar.* Readers of this book will enjoy the satisfying answers to the riddles of life that only authentic Kabbalah provides. Travel through the pages and prepare for an astonishing journey into the Upper Worlds.

Introduction to the Book of Zohar

This volume, along with *The Science of Kabbalah,* is a required preparation for those who wish to understand the hidden message of *The Book of Zohar.* Among the many helpful topics dealt with in this text is an introduction to the "language of roots and branches," without which the stories in *The Zohar* are mere fable and legend. Introduction to *The Book of Zohar* will provide readers with the necessary tools to understand authentic Kabbalah as it was originally meant to be—as a means to attain the Upper Worlds.

The Kabbalist: a cinematic novel

At the dawn of the deadliest era in human history, the 20th century, a mysterious man appeared carrying a stern warning for humanity and an unlikely solution to its suffering. In his writings, Kabbalist Yehuda Ashlag described in clarity and great detail the wars and upheavals he foresaw, and even more strikingly, the current economic, political, and social crises we are facing today. His deep yearning for a united humanity has driven him to unlock *The Book of Zohar* and make it—and the unique force contained therein—accessible to all.

The Kabbalist is a cinematic novel that will turn on its head everything you thought you knew about Kabbalah, spirituality, freedom of will, and our perception of reality. The book carries a message of unity with scientific clarity and poetic depth. It transcends religion, nationality, mysticism, and the fabric of space and time to show us that the only miracle is the one taking place within, when we begin to act in harmony with Nature and with the entire humanity.

A Sage's Fruit: essays of Baal HaSulam

For over sixty years, some of the most powerful essays written by Rav Yehuda Ashlag, known as Baal HaSulam (Owner of the Ladder) for his *Sulam* (Ladder) commentary on *The Book of Zohar*, have been sealed and concealed. Owing to the poor state of the manuscripts you will find some ellipses because the original text is incomplete, and because it cannot be read with certainty.

And yet, the content and message resonate from every page in this inspiring book. You cannot truly understand Baal HaSulam until you read such seminal essays as "600,000 Souls," "Exile and Redemption," or "One Commandment."

A Sage's Fruit: letters of Baal HaSulam

When the great Kabbalist, Rav Yehuda Leib Halevi Ashlag, author of the *Sulam* (Ladder) commentary on *The Book of Zohar*, had to travel, he would write elaborate letters to his students, providing them with guidance and encouragement. These letters reveal the special relationships cultivated between the great teacher and his students. *A Sage's Fruit: letters of Baal HaSulam* is a compilation of those letters. The unique style and tone that Rav Ashlag uses here offer inspiration and guidance to any seeker of spiritual advancement. Now that they are out, it is unclear how we could perceive spiritual advancement without them.

CONTACT INFORMATION

1057 Steeles Avenue West, Suite 532

Toronto, ON, M2R 3X1

Canada

Bnei Baruch USA,

2009 85th street, #51,

Brooklyn, New York, 11214

USA

E-mail: info@kabbalah.info

Web site: www.kabbalah.info

Toll free in USA and Canada:

1-866-LAITMAN

Fax: 1-905 886 9697